A MURDERER'S GUIDE TO CLEANING

A MURDERER'S GUIDE TO CLEANING

And Other Stories From My Life As A Probation Officer

ELIZABETH BAXTER

A Oneworld Book

First published by Oneworld Publications Ltd in 2026

Copyright © Elizabeth Baxter, 2026

The moral right of Elizabeth Baxter to be identified as the Author of this work has been asserted by her in accordance with the Copyright, Designs, and Patents Act 1988

All rights reserved
Copyright under Berne Convention
A CIP record for this title is available from the British Library

ISBN 978-1-83643-167-1
eISBN 978-1-83643-168-8

Typeset by Geethik Technologies
Printed and bound in Great Britain by Clays Ltd, Elcograf S.p.A.

No part of this publication may be reproduced, stored in a retrieval system, or transmitted, in any form or by any means, electronic, mechanical, photocopying, recording or otherwise, or used in any manner for the purpose of training artificial intelligence technologies or systems, without the prior permission of the publishers.

The authorised representative in the EEA is eucomply OU,
Pärnu mnt 139b-14, 11317 Tallinn, Estonia
(email: hello@eucompliancepartner.com / phone: +33757690241)

Oneworld Publications Ltd
10 Bloomsbury Street
London WC1B 3SR
England

Stay up to date with the latest books,
special offers, and exclusive content from
Oneworld with our newsletter

Sign up on our website
oneworld.co.uk

Contents

Preface		xi
Introduction: Now		xv
1	Back Then	1
2	Steve	15
3	Stella	29
4	Jake	47
5	Adam	61
6	Chantelle	77
7	George	93
8	Abdul	109
9	Maisy	121
10	Andrew	137
11	Luke	157
12	Lenny	175
13	Petra	191
14	Liz	207
15	What Probation Is Like Now	225
Acknowledgements		251

To all Probation Officers. Unsung heroes.
When things go wrong, you're the first to be blamed.
When things go right, you're the
first to be forgotten.

And especially to Dave. We trained together,
but when I couldn't stand it anymore, I left.
You and many others stayed.
This is for you.

Due to the sensitive nature of the topics discussed, real names and uniquely identifying characteristics of most individuals in this book have been changed to maintain their anonymity. In order to protect their privacy, some individuals are composites of multiple people with whom the author worked.

Preface

As I write, there are around 241,540 offenders supervised by 21,022 members of Probation Service staff in the UK. Of those staff only 5,657 are qualified Probation Officers.*†

The Probation Service was born from a religious belief that criminals could be redeemed if they were treated with kindness and compassion. Founded in 1907, the service was mostly run by missionaries on a voluntary basis until the Criminal Justice Act of 1948 introduced probation as an alternative to prison, preserving the central ethos of compassion and rehabilitation. Up until the mid-1990s, Probation Officers worked under the motto of 'Advise. Assist. Befriend',

---

*   *Offender management statistics quarterly: October to December 2024*, HM Prison & Probation Service, 24 April 2025: https://www.gov.uk/government/statistics/offender-management-statistics-quarterly-april-to-june-2024/offender-management-statistics-quarterly-april-to-june-2024.

†   *HM Prison and Probation Service workforce quarterly: March 2025*, HM Prison & Probation Service, 15 May 2025: https://www.gov.uk/government/statistics/hm-prison-and-probation-service-workforce-quarterly-march-2025/hm-prison-and-probation-service-workforce-quarterly-march-2025.

offering a remedial approach to offenders. All Probation Officers trained as social workers. By the late 1990s there was a shift in ethos, reflected in a new motto: 'Public Protection, Enforcement and Rehabilitation'. The training moved away from social work and towards something more specialist and punitive. The Criminal Justice Act of 2003 reinforced this. The Probation Service is the only criminal justice department that works with offenders from their initial court appearance, through every sentence, both in the community and in custody, right through to parole. In view of this, many long-term Probation Officers have worked with the same people for years, getting to know everything about them. My longest relationship with a client spanned twenty years.

While this has now changed, Probation Officers used to come from all walks of life, each with personal reasons for wanting to work with criminals. Some came from businesses that employ offenders, some were victims of crime, others were ex-criminals themselves – but all were possessed by a social conscience and a desire to help people change for the better. A significant majority attended university as mature students and nearly all had a rich pool of prior life experience to draw upon. Given their range of backgrounds, probation workers most closely represented those within the criminal justice system.

The Probation Service had a decent track record of supervising offenders but, despite this, the then-Justice Secretary Chris Grayling went against all advice given by criminal justice departments and charities and part-privatised the service in 2014. The service was then split into two sectors: the National Probation Service remained within the public sector and was responsible for high-risk offenders, and the Community Rehabilitation Companies (CRCs) were sold to private companies and made responsible for managing low- and medium-risk offenders.

Privatisation was a disaster. Staff were overstretched and underqualified, risk assessments were not carried out properly and the categorisation of high- versus low-risk offenders was routinely muddled. HM Inspectorate of Probation eventually concluded that the private companies had failed to properly assess the risk of harm in *half* of all cases. To cut costs, some junior staff were left supervising up to 200 offenders – absolute capacity is supposed to be sixty. Thousands of offenders were supervised with one phone call every six weeks rather than regular face-to-face contact. There were steady rounds of redundancies, meaning remaining staff were so overworked and stressed they also left in droves. Poor pay and inadequate conditions made it impossible to replace the experienced officers who had left. The private companies also lost money, needing to be bailed out to the tune of £342 million. None of that went towards extra staff.

As a result of Grayling's amendments, the National Probation Service maintained their good record as before, while in the CRCs serious crimes committed by people on probation rose by twenty per cent.* As the then-HM Chief Inspector of Probation Dame Glenys Stacey said at the time, 'These services

---

* Lizzie Dearden, 'Government's privatisation of probation services "putting public at risk" as offenders monitored by phone', *Independent*, 14 December 2017: https://www.independent.co.uk/news/uk/home-news/probation-services-failing-privatisation-model-two-tier-system-risks-murderer-sexual-offences-a8108591.html.

aren't very visible, but they really do matter… neglected prisoners are more likely to reoffend.'

Following some high-profile serious offences by people on probation and the subsequent backlash in 2021, the probation system was re-unified under the National Probation Service. However, it has yet to recover. Probation Officers on the ground report significant staff shortages and an alarming lack of experience.

From the outset, experts agreed that privatisation was reckless, but the government went ahead anyway. It was a dangerous and expensive mistake. Particularly unnerving, given the criminal justice system is all about consequences, is the fact 'Failing Grayling' went on to waste vast amounts of public money on other stupid ideas as Secretary of State for Transport before being elevated to the House of Lords. Currently, rather than mature officers with life experience and a vocation to work in probation, many new Probation Officers are fresh from sixth form and a Criminology degree, having never heard of probation before they went to university. A large majority are young white women who lack the requisite life experience.

This book is about those halcyon days before privatisation when officers had the time and experience to make a difference. I spent twenty-five years of my life doing a job I felt really mattered. I hope, in reading this book, you will agree.

Introduction

Now

I look down at the woman in the photographs on my desk. Her face is swollen and purple with bruises, and large finger marks bracket her neck. The neighbours had heard her begging him to stop. 'Why are you doing this to me?' she pleaded as his fist collided with her face again.

'Because I can,' he replied.

I take a deep breath before opening the manila file containing the rest of the evidence. It's his first appointment with me. There are witness statements from his wife and the neighbours and a transcript of his police interview.

At the top is the list of charges:

> Assault – Actual Bodily Harm (ABH)
> Controlling or Coercive Behaviour in an Intimate or Family Relationship Section 76
> Assault Police Officer

Another wife-beater.

It's January and we're deep in our annual, post-Christmas run of domestic violence.

I scan the interview room for a moment, eyes settling on the rips in the orange hessian wallpaper. It has adorned the walls since the Queen opened the probation office in 1974. I feel a familiar twinge of embarrassment at meeting a new client in such a squalid room. The bare desk, the hard plastic chairs, the bright white strip light that exposes every wrinkle on my face.

I try to conjure an image of what he's going to look like, how he will behave. He will likely argue that he is innocent. He will try and belittle me. I call him in from the waiting room, 'Mr Brown? Would you like to come through?'

Mr Brown is a good-looking man in his forties. He is wearing a suit and carrying a briefcase. The ones in suits are usually the worst, so I brace myself. If you passed him in the street, you wouldn't think twice – an unremarkable, decent sort. The scent, however, gives him away. He is coated in so much cheap body spray that he smells like a teenage boy.

Before I have the chance to even introduce myself, he announces, 'I expressly asked for a man.'

I was right, I think. *Making demands already.*

Meeting his gaze, I continue: 'Mr Brown, I'm very sorry for your disappointment, but you have just been made the subject of a Probation Order by the court. I'm afraid you can't choose who supervises you. However, if you don't want this Order, I'm quite happy to take the matter back to court, where I'm sure they wouldn't mind imposing a custodial sentence instead.'

That'll shut him up.

'No need for that,' says Mr Brown, who suddenly looks perturbed. 'I'll just have to put up with you.'

He flashes a broad smile, which he clearly thinks is charming.

'Let's start again, shall we Mr Brown? My name is Elizabeth Baxter. I'm an experienced Probation Officer and over the next few months we are going to work together to explore how you found yourself here and try to make sure you don't find yourself in the same situation again.'

'I got into this situation because of my bitch of a wife,' he hisses.

The word *bitch* makes my stomach lurch. He wants to make me uncomfortable, but I've heard so much worse. Now I only experience intense irritation. I sigh and adopt my best 'you won't get the better of me' look.

'Yes, well, Mr Brown. There's no need for that kind of language is there? We'll be talking in more detail about *your* offending behaviour as we get into the Order.'

His lips tighten into a narrow scowl. This is not a promising start. I've got to see this man every week for nine months, then once a month for the next three. Together, we must try to change his attitude towards women and do our best to ensure he doesn't hit one again.

I'm going to have my work cut out.

I think about his wife – scared in her own home, unable to leave him, mortified that other people might discover the truth. Will she have the courage to go? Or are there parts of him she still loves? I don't know her but I want to protect her.

'Mr Brown, your wife sustained a number of injuries when you punched her. I've been reading the witness statement, and I note that she was very upset after you knocked her to the ground. You simply stepped over her, straightened your tie and spent several minutes looking at yourself in the mirror.'

I pause for a moment and look him straight in the eye.

'What did you see, Mr Brown?'

***

I leave the interview room an hour later, dreaming of coffee, and bump into my colleague Mick in the corridor.

'How was yours?' he enquires.

'Arsehole,' I reply. 'But one day I might find a nice Mr Brown in there.'

'Still an optimist?'

For a moment I see the photographs again, the finger-marks in bruised flesh. I shake it off. 'I'll tell you in a year.'

You see, Probation Officers are different to others working in the criminal justice system. We have to see *past* the arsehole, to what could be. The officers who arrested Mr Brown would have thought he was an arsehole because they'd caught him assaulting his wife; and quickly confirmed this when he punched one of them while resisting arrest.

The solicitor who represented him will also think he's an arsehole – she has only met him twice and had to listen to all the feeble excuses he made for beating up his wife. Nevertheless, she will do her best to persuade the court that Mr Brown isn't *that* much of an arsehole, even though she clearly thinks he is.

Members of the court will think he's an arsehole. They've never spoken to him directly, but they see people exactly like him in court every single day.

But I will spend *months* with Mr Brown, listening to his justifications and then unpicking them with him. I will uncover whether he behaves like an arsehole because of his upbringing, circumstances or some other reason. I might find that he's not a complete arsehole after all, in which case I can help him change. And if he turns out to just be an arsehole, I can help to facilitate strategies to protect his wife and the public.

Just as with all my other clients – the burglars, the arsonists, the rapists – I'll be looking for that small chink of humanity and trying to draw it to the fore.

While the following stories revolve around criminals, they aren't about crime. They are about people, often very vulnerable ones, and what working with them has taught me. It's about how it felt doing the school run and tidying up after my husband and children after a day spent with murderers and paedophiles.

1

Back Then

Even a sensible girl can end up on the wrong side of the law.

I am the well-behaved, only child of a quiet and responsible couple and enjoyed a sheltered upbringing. I've got white-blonde hair and a mouth that is too big for my face. At school I am routinely known as 'rubber lips'.

As a teenager I'd spend my time sitting in my bedroom reading Danielle Steel and dreaming of romance and adventure. My father worked in the local factory and would come home to my mother, the *Daily Telegraph* pressed into his hands, and would hide behind it all evening; I hardly ever actually saw his face, except when he exchanged the newspaper for the evening news.

Our house was quiet. I never once heard my parents argue, not even whispered disputes after I'd gone to bed. I figured this was normal. I'd never given much thought to violence or abuse – I thought things like that only happened in soap operas.

It was the early eighties. A lot was going on in the country: inflation was way up, the Brixton riots soon erupted and the miners' strikes followed, but I had no interest in any of it. When I left home, aged seventeen, I knew nothing about politics and couldn't make a cup of tea.

I'd never contemplated a 'career'. It was my mother's firm wish that I would marry a rich farmer and have children by the age of twenty-five, after which I'd proceed to wait upon my family's every need. To achieve this goal, she constantly corrected my grammar and erased as many signs of a regional accent as she could. So, despite living on the same council estate as my friends, I was known as 'the posh girl' (with rubber lips).

I loved going round to other people's houses – the chaos, noise and laughter. My best friend's house always smelled of brown sauce, they ate spam and were always making jokes. (There was rarely laughter in our quiet house and I certainly wasn't allowed spam). Their Christmases were raucous while I wasn't allowed to believe in Santa because it was 'stupid'. They went to Butlin's on holiday; our Ford Anglia was covered in National Trust stickers. During school holidays my parents would pack the car with a tent and sandwiches, and we would traverse the country, visiting every castle they could find in an effort to progress my education. How I longed for Butlin's…

So, at the very first opportunity, I left home to share a house with friends. I can still recall my mother's horrified protestations about how I wouldn't cope. Of course, she was right. But I was seventeen and thought I knew everything.

Even though I'd seen some nice National Trust houses in my youth, I wasn't exactly prepared for life and expectations were low. I wasn't sure how to meet the farmer of my mother's dreams so upon leaving school I became a dental nurse. I liked it well enough, but I got bored quickly. At one point, the dentist I assisted went on a weekend introductory course on plastic surgery and decided to practise on my lips upon his return. I held the mirror in one hand and the suction machine in the other. He clamped my lips back, slit the skin between my lips and my gums, removed the fat and stitched me back up. I watched with morbid fascination through the whole procedure.

A new life was unfolding before me. I was no longer 'rubber lips'. I'd escaped my parents and was hosting parties with new friends. Suddenly, I was popular and cool. I had the noisy, chaotic, 'grown-up' house I'd always craved – even if our mums still delivered dinner and came round regularly to do the housework. I felt free.

My first year of freedom passed uneventfully. We'd just about mastered how to cook the basics and relished our favourite meal, affectionately known as 'Ghetto Surprise' – a concoction of beans, tomato soup, spam and white bread, which we all pretended to like (while secretly praying for a food delivery from someone's mother).

Then one day everything changed.

We'd been to the pub and were throwing an impromptu party at ours after. It was a bit different to normal. At some point the party became overrun by strangers. They all seemed nice enough, so we allowed them to stay.

Two of the gatecrashers, Kelvin and Dan, arrived with dope. Before this, I'd never taken drugs in my life, nor had any of my housemates. They were an imposing pair, both large skinheads. Kelvin had an unusually big skull and almost no neck, while Dan showcased the dazed, rolling eyes of the perpetually stoned. Nevertheless, when they cheerfully passed the dope around, we thought we'd try it so we didn't seem rude or wimpy. After just two puffs, my best friend and I scuffled to bed where we were sick into a wicker bin, though most of it landed in our own hands and on the floor.

Soon Kelvin and Dan became regulars. I never smoked dope again and continued to be the goody-goody I'd always been.

What would later emerge was that they were well-known drug dealers. They'd been in prison on numerous occasions for a variety of other offences too, including burglary and assault. After a few weeks of weekend parties they tried to persuade me to steal drugs from work. As far as I was aware, there were no drugs in the dental surgery, but Kelvin and Dan informed me there were opiates in the anaesthetic that the dentist used and that they could sell it. I wondered who on earth would use the stuff deliberately, as it only made your face go numb, and declined.

But soon they were meeting me near work. Every day they'd be at the bus stop, waiting. I smiled at them but I was terrified. I wanted to go back home to my parents, but I couldn't tell anyone. The two big friendly lads from our parties had morphed into men, twice my size, intimidating me at work.

They continued to harass me for drugs but, fighting my persistent compulsion to please, I refused. I should have informed the dentist but wasn't sure how to explain how I knew a pair of drug-dealers. I could have told the police but saying two 'friends' met me at work every day felt a bit feeble, even if I was petrified. So, one day, when the dentist asked me to dispose of a box full of out-of-date phials of anaesthetic,

I seized my chance. I could get these guys off my back and solve the problem. I figured the anaesthetic wouldn't work because it was old, so nobody would want it or get hurt, and Kelvin and Dan would be on their merry way. So, instead of taking the box to the chemist to dispose of I gave it to the boys. Job done.

A week later I was arrested for Possession and Supply of a Class A drug. A serious charge for a girl who had never so much as shoplifted sweets from Woolworths.

As soon as I'd heard the loud knock on the door, I knew. Given the dread I'd felt for most of that week, it was almost a relief to be found out.

The police asked if I knew why they were there, and I admitted everything straight away. They weren't unkind, but I was intimidated by them. I'd never spoken to a police officer before. They said they were going to put handcuffs on me to take me to the police station to question me further. I begged them not to put cuffs on, I was so worried about the neighbours seeing. It was humiliating enough being arrested let alone anyone watching. They agreed not to put them on and chatted amiably. In the back of the police car, I sat flanked by two officers – small, scared and ludicrously squashed.

My stomach gripped by the tightest of knots, my mouth dry and my head spinning, I was marched into the custody suite and checked in. All the time my mind was racing – what was going to happen? They put me in a cell and locked the door. I wanted to go home.

The place reeked of cigarettes and sweat. I lay down on the hard bench and cried. It was only early evening, but I felt drained. Shortly afterwards I was taken for questioning. They asked if I wanted a solicitor. I just wanted to get it over with, so I said no. I gave them all the details. In fact, I couldn't wait to tell them. I wanted to get it off my chest. Afterwards they took me back to the cell. Kelvin and Dan were also in the cells and Dan was looking out of the spy hole in his door as we walked past and he started shouting:

'Lizzie! Did you tell them anything?'

I never thought about them when I was telling the police *everything*.

'No,' I said, 'nothing at all.'

Oh shit.

'That's what I like to hear, Lizzie.'

It was cold in the cell. Trembling, and scared – mostly of Dan and Kelvin and what they might do if they knew I'd talked – I curled into a ball and drifted into sleep.

Eventually, the Sergeant came in for a chat. He said I was the same age as his daughter. He asked if I wanted a tour around the police station and later gave me a lift home. I was so disorientated but, in that moment, I knew I'd rather have them as friends than Kelvin and Dan.

As soon as I got home, I got in the bath to wash away my shame. Mid-soak, I had a distinct feeling of excitement. During the tour around the police station, I had seen women officers not much older than me discussing criminals and taking notes with their male counterparts. There had been such a strong sense of camaraderie in the room. *I'd like to be a police officer,* I thought. DS Lamb, who had arrested me, had said that in the future, once my conviction had been spent, I could apply. I thought it was just a throwaway comment when he said it, but maybe I really could. It was a revelation.

A few weeks later, on a sunny afternoon, I was standing in the dock at the local magistrate's court in my best Laura Ashley dress looking angelic. Appearing alongside Kelvin and Dan, I felt particularly small. I didn't look at them, keeping my eyes forward, hoping they wouldn't notice I was there. They were soon taken away by men with jangling keys hanging from their belts. I looked down at my clenched knuckles and waited for my turn.

I am an eighteen-year-old goody-two-shoes. I still read Smash Hits. *I can't believe I'm here. Bad people go to prison. Not me.*

The duty solicitor stood up. I'd only met him in court that day. 'Elizabeth Baxter is of previous good character,' he said briskly. 'She accepted responsibility for her part in this offence immediately. In my view she is unlikely to abscond. I would ask the court to consider bail.'

I stood in the dock, shaking. I couldn't breathe. Staring up at the magistrates, I willed them to let me out. It felt like an eternity standing there watching them shuffle papers before one looked down at me and said:

'I'm minded to impose bail but I want to know more about you before I sentence you, so we'll adjourn for three weeks for a PSR.'

I had absolutely no idea what they were talking about, but I heard the word bail and that was enough for me. I could breathe again.

Outside the court room, a Captain Birdseye lookalike approached me. He was wearing a checked shirt and corduroy trousers and seemed considerably more relaxed than the black-suited solicitors in the court.

He held his hand out.

'Hello Elizabeth, my name is Mick and I'm a Probation Officer and blimey, I don't think I've ever seen anyone look so scared in my life! You can calm down. I won't bite.'

He explained to me that he was going to write a report for the court called a Pre-Sentence Report (PSR). He said he would be reading the witness statements, and interviewing me about why I committed the offence, if I regretted it, what kind of life I led, and my background, and then, based on that, he would recommend the sentence that the court should impose upon me.

Still sick with nerves, I barely understood what he was saying and I vacantly watched his mouth move, desperate to run away. Mick gave me an appointment for the following week.

The seven days felt interminable. I arrived at the Probation office in a grey pinafore dress that I had chosen as I thought it made me look both smart and innocent, though I must have looked like an overgrown schoolgirl.

Mick called me into the office, a spartan place with bright orange hessian wallpaper punctuated by yellowing posters and leaflets stuck to the wall with drawing pins. There was a bare desk in the middle and two chairs either side. The strip lighting above the desk was so bright it made me want to shut my eyes. I couldn't believe I was there.

'You've really got yourself in the shit here haven't you, Elizabeth, or should I call you Lizzie?' Mick said. He must have seen the shock on my face and threw me a calm, kind smile. 'Don't worry, you'll be all right. Tell me all about what happened.'

I took a deep breath. I laugh when I'm nervous and had spent the morning fretting that I would just start giggling and Mick would think I considered the whole interview a joke. In the end, I lurched straight into regaling him with the full details of my crime, why I'd done it, how terrible I felt afterwards. I told him about my sensible parents and school and how I'd never get into trouble ever again.

Mick said that the offence was serious enough for me to go to prison. I nearly shat myself. As it was my first offence, that wasn't likely, he told me. I breathed a sigh of relief. Meanwhile, Dan and Kelvin were sure to get long custodial sentences as repeat offenders; to be frank, I was relieved I wouldn't have to see them again. Mick said that he was going to recommend that I have a Probation Order and see him every week. I liked the idea. I was surprised that Probation Officers were important enough to influence sentencing. In fact, I'd never really heard of Probation Officers until then.

When I was sentenced, the court was full of people in suits whispering among themselves. I wondered why they were all there, whether they were whispering about me, but then I noticed one of them chuckling. I could see that it was a normal day for them. It felt like the most abnormal day in the world to me.

Suddenly a loud voice rang out.

'Elizabeth Baxter! Look at me!'

I looked up at the magistrate. She looked severe and I wanted to turn away, but she had told me to look at her, so I did. I couldn't think properly. I was anxious that if I stared into her face she'd tell me off, so I stared intently at the tight bun perched on the top of her head.

'You have committed a very serious offence,' she said sternly. 'I could send you to prison.'

I could feel the blood draining from my face. The palms of my hands were wet. I wanted to wee.

The magistrate paused weightily, her expression unreadable. *Please no...*

'But I've listened to what your Probation Officer recommended and I'm going to be lenient,' she said. 'I am making you the subject of a two-year Probation Order, do you understand?'

I nodded in agreement with her. I wanted to cry with relief and could feel my chin quivering as I gulped back tears.

'Now, young lady, what do you want to do with yourself in the future?'

The magistrate's expression had softened, and she was smiling at me encouragingly. I said the first thing that popped into my head.

'I'd like to help people.'

'Well, I hope that one day you will. I don't want to see you in my court again; do you hear me?'

For the next few months, Mick was a regular feature in my life. We talked about how I'd gotten into trouble, but it was soon clear to him that I was unlikely to do it again, both because I wasn't inherently dishonest, but also because he continually joked that I was the most petrified person he'd ever seen in court.

As a result of my offence, I'd been sacked from the dentist and Mick asked what job I would like to do instead.

'I'd like to join the police force,' I replied.

'You're mad!' he said. 'Be a Probation Officer if you want to work with criminals! You don't have to work shifts, you don't get beaten up and you really get to know people, like I have you. In some cases, you can help people who have been criminals for years to change. It's the most rewarding job in the world.'

'I think I'd like that,' I said.

'Then keep your nose clean, get some relevant work experience, go to night school, and you might end up as one of my colleagues. I also think you need to get some actual, real-life experience, see how some people are forced to live.'

***

It was the 1980s; unemployment was high and the chances of getting decent work were low. Mick had suggested I talk to his friend Ray, who was the manager of a local drop-in centre for the unemployed.

Ray was on a mission to ensure that all the young people he met got a job. Thankfully, he made me one of his 'projects'. I started on reception as a volunteer, but Ray encouraged me to undertake training so I could go further. By the time I was twenty, I was a Welfare Rights Worker, an expert in social security benefits. I was being paid and I felt valuable. I was representing claimants at tribunals. I was a trade union youth rep travelling to other parts of the country helping the families of striking miners get the money they were entitled to. I was on committees. I felt like I'd been asleep before and suddenly I was awake. I watched the news, read every paper. I would argue with anyone who liked Margaret Thatcher, particularly my dad, who would roll his eyes in frustration and return to his *Telegraph*. I no longer wanted to go to Butlin's and you wouldn't catch me dead in a castle, seeing as they were built on the backs of the working classes. I had an opinion and I liked it.

Frankly, I was a pain in the arse.

I'd never realised before how liberating it was to have an opinion and be able to join the conversation. Ray was an inspiration who believed that anyone could achieve anything if they really wanted to. This was in complete contrast to what I had been told at school, that I'd never amount to much. He made me feel confident and I learned that one person's belief in you can influence your whole life. It's a skill I've tried to bring into my own practice.

It was Ray who suggested to the Probation Service that I could go into prisons to advise prisoners about benefit claims pre-release and help them build some life skills that would give them a small fighting chance once on the outside. Sometimes I'd see Mick and he would smile and look pleased with himself because of my progress.

Ten years of working, night school and university later and I was a Probation Officer.

Mick was waiting for me on my first day on the job. I hadn't seen him for a few years and he *really* looked like Captain Birdseye now, with silver curly hair and grey beard. He was still in a checked shirt and corduroy trousers though.

'You did it, Lizzie! I'm going to take you to your new office.'

We went in. The 'interior designer' clearly *loved* orange. It was still everywhere, as though you were trapped in a Sainsbury's bag. Even splattered with those yellowing, dog-eared leaflets, it looked glorious to me.

There were two desks, one piled high with files and the other empty. Mick pointed to the empty desk and said, 'That one's yours.' He sat down at the other one. 'This one is mine.'

'We're sharing an office?'

'Yes!'

I was ecstatic and hugged Mick. He too was beaming.

'I'm going to be your mentor. I knew you could do it!'

My first caseload included burglars, a prostitute, sex offenders, a drug dealer and various violent offenders. My eyes rested upon the file of a murderer, 'Steve'. He had been in the system for so long that he had more than one file to his name. They were thick and full of carefully written notes by the various officers who had worked with him over the years. The files included a pile of letters from his anguished mother who couldn't believe what her gentle son had done and worried about how he would cope in prison. She'd asked probation for updates, and they'd written to each other regularly. I saw in the notes that his mother had died, and the last Probation Officer had gone to the funeral and seen Steve there, standing next to his mother's grave in handcuffs. Though the write-up remained professional, there was a hint of pity in the Probation Officer's account.

I was surprised to get a murderer straight away, but after reading his files, I felt a certain familiarity. I couldn't wait to meet him for myself. He had already been incarcerated for twenty years and would be a different person to the one who had committed the murder. Assessed as low risk, he was the first person I saw on my own, without Mick.

2

Steve

Steve and his wife, Julie, had spent the day in the pub. They were already very drunk and carried on drinking at home. Steve remembers that, initially, Julie was excitable, jovial, talking loudly and dancing around the kitchen with the radio blaring in the background. But her mood changed and she became angry, shouting at him. He described how she got louder and louder and that she was right 'in his face', shouting and poking him in the chest. Quickly sobering up, he didn't retaliate at first and just calmly asked her to stop. She carried on, poking him more and getting closer, goading him. He described how this kind of behaviour was not uncharacteristic and admitted that he had hit her before when she had refused to quiet down, but previously she had hit him back and he felt that the ensuing fights had been relatively equal. This would be a precursor to sex, followed by sleep and an apology to each other the following day. He expected a similar scenario this night, but somehow, he felt different, he couldn't stand it any longer. He just wanted her to stop.

When the police arrived, Julie was pronounced dead at the scene. Steve had called them, he hadn't tried to hide what he had done or move her body, but one thing was noticeable: the kitchen was spotless, no blood, no mess. Nothing.

The murder described in the file was bland, cold, factual. Nevertheless, the crime was brutal.

***

I'm nervous. My hand sweats as I grip the briefcase I use to look important. I am venturing where most people don't. Prison. It's as though I'm journeying further and further from reality. The sounds of cars, of daily life, gradually disappear, replaced by the shouts and heckles of inmates and the clanging of doors. There is a cacophony of sound, none of it familiar. It is hard to believe that the city is carrying on as usual outside the walls, oblivious to this other society. A distinctive cabbage-like smell floods the place – BO and feet offset by artificial pine disinfectant. Calls of 'Miss! Who have you come to see?' Everyone's curious about this new face on the wing; anything to puncture the perpetual boredom of prison life. My exhilaration is tinged with trepidation – I am a professional woman about to interview a murderer. In the years that have elapsed since that day, the feeling of intrigue and nervousness when meeting a new client has never worn off, though the sounds and smells of the prison are now familiar.

Steve is waiting in the interview room, sitting next to a small, barred window, the shadow painting stripes across his face. He looks up at me but does not make eye contact.

Introducing myself, I explain that I'm his new Probation Officer.

'I was quite happy with Pat, the old one,' he mutters, and is silent again, still refusing to look at me.

Immediately, I apologise.

'I'm sorry, Pat has retired, so it'll be me that sees you from now on. Your next parole hearing is in three years, so we've got plenty of time to get to know each other. You could tell me about the offence straight away, get it over with. Tell me everything and anything, what you did. How you felt.'

I am conscious that I don't say the word murder out loud. He looks resigned. He must regurgitate the details for every Parole Board hearing and every time he gets a new Probation Officer, plenty of times over the twenty years he has been locked up.

He knows I'll be assessing him for parole and looking to see if those many years in prison have rendered him safe to be released. His last parole application was turned down due to an apparent lack of remorse.

I want to find out how he really feels about what he did.

Opening his file on the desk between us, I delve into the background information recorded by my predecessors. I find an entry by Pat, his last Officer, which I offer to read out to him. He nods in agreement.

'"Steve describes himself as a timid man. He told me that he lacked the confidence and argumentative nature of his wife and that sometimes he felt completely overpowered by her. He was unable to verbally challenge her, and she would goad him into an argument that he couldn't win. He could never compete with her verbal altercations, so violence had felt like his way of evening things out. He described being deeply unhappy within the relationship but felt that his wife had complete control over him and therefore believed that he was unable to leave her."' I pause. 'Does this still feel right to you, Steve?'

He nods but still doesn't look at me.

'Steve, could you describe to me what happened on that night please? Try to be as detailed as you can, and include your feelings, as this will all help me and eventually the Parole Board to understand when the time comes.'

Steve takes a deep breath.

'Okay then. We'd been in the pub all day. I can't even remember if it was a good day. We went home and Julie started shouting, which was normal when she'd had a few.

'I asked her to keep her voice down and she told me to piss off and said she could do what she liked. She started shouting in my face and poking me, she knew I didn't like it if she was up too close, so I pushed her away. It wasn't a strong push, more of a nudge. Then she put the radio on loud and started to shout over the top – she knew I didn't like loud noises, so she did it to wind me up.

'I couldn't think straight, all that racket, and she was back in my face again, so I pushed her away harder, and she started screaming and punching me. I just wanted her to be quiet and have some peace. I was begging her to stop shouting. I turned the radio off, but she just laughed – not a nice laugh, a spiteful one. We were standing in the kitchen, and I looked around for anything to stop her from shouting at me. The frying pan was on the cooker, so I just grabbed it and hit her over the head. I didn't even think first, I was just desperate for some quiet. I had an instant feeling of relief.

'The pan just seemed to bounce off her and she looked shocked. Cold sausages flew across the kitchen; I felt a bit annoyed because the gravy splashed the cupboards – we should have finished those sausages before we went out and I could have washed the pan. Anyway, she looked at me and screamed and I thought *she's still not being quiet*, so I hit her again. She carried on looking at me, her mouth was moving, but only groans were coming out. It was nice that it was a bit quieter.

'There was some blood coming out of her eye and she put her hands in front of her face. It felt better when she couldn't stare at me, and she was quiet. I was thankful to have some peace. I didn't want her to shout at me anymore, so I kept on hitting her over the head. I could feel the vibrations of the pan bouncing off her going up my arm. It felt quite soothing, so I got into a rhythm with it. It sounded a bit like African drumming, so I imagined I was there. Apart from that, there was no other noise. I felt peaceful but also excited about the peace. She was on the ground by this time. It was hurting my back bending over, so I stopped. I knew she was dead. I felt cold inside, empty, not peaceful anymore, but kind of calm. I looked around the kitchen, there was blood everywhere and some gravy. I don't like mess, so I thought I'd clean it up before I called the police.'

I try not to look shocked as he tells me this. He has displayed almost no emotion. I keep my face professional and impassive. I'm not sure what to say, so I ask: 'How did you clean it up?'

Steve's face lights up.

'Well, first I got paper towels and put those around her on the floor. They weren't enough to soak the blood up and it all came through, but I knew I shouldn't move her as the police would want to know exactly what went on. The paper towels blotted the blood a bit, but it carried on spreading around the floor. When I picked up the paper towels they dripped then fell apart. Luckily, we had some black bin liners, so I put them in there. Then I looked in the cupboards to see what I could use to get the blood off the tiles and the grouting – it had splattered quite a bit and some of it was mixed with gravy. I saw some Persil, so I used some of that and made it into a paste. I wiped the tiles first, then scrubbed them with the paste and used Julie's toothbrush to clean the grouting, as she wouldn't be needing it anymore. It really did come up lovely.'

As I watch Steve animatedly describe how he cleaned the grouting I immediately understand why his last parole application was turned down. He displayed not a shred of remorse. I nod at him encouragingly to carry on. He still doesn't look at me but continues to talk.

'After the Persil paste, I used Ajax and then Flash spray because those smell nice and create a shine rather than a smear. I'd heard that vinegar works well too, so I used a bit of that. All the blood was gone. It was more difficult on the floor because I didn't want to disturb her body, and there was a lot of blood, so I had no choice. It was a shame to ruin the towels, but I needed something to blot the blood. I put the towels all around her to soak it up, then put those in bin bags, so it wouldn't drip. I mopped the floor; I used cola this time mixed with Persil as I'd heard that's good for floors, and it worked! Julie didn't like me trying new cleaning methods, so it was nice to go in the cupboards and use things she wouldn't have agreed to. I was respectful and didn't bash into her with the mop. Julie didn't like being tidy. It was the best I'd ever seen the kitchen look. The only bit of mess was her being on the floor. When the police came, it was spotless. I was quite satisfied.'

I'm stunned into silence. Steve stops talking and waits for me to respond. I can't think what to say. What exactly can you say to a man who's proudly told you about the cleaning products he's used after killing his wife? So I simply tell him that I'll come back next week. On the way out I ask the prison staff if I can see him in his cell next time. They agree.

His cell is sparkling. Though tiny, there isn't a thing out of place. Steve has managed to make it look nice, almost homely. He is a trusted lifer, so he has a kettle and makes me a cup of tea. After I finish it, I notice that he gives the cup an extra scrub.

'How do you keep your cell so clean?' I ask.

Steve flashes me a conspiratorial look and whispers, 'I mix Marmite and bread until it ferments into alcohol, then drain the alcohol off. The other prisoners drink it, but I use it to clean my taps. I mix cola and washing powder for the floor. I can't get Persil now, so I just use what the prison gives me, but I don't know what make it is. I use a prison flip-flop to buff it afterwards and to get any fluff up. I use that on my taps too to make them shine. I've never felt clean since that day, you know. Having a clean cell helps.'

***

I see Steve regularly over the following three years until his next parole hearing, and really get to know him and how he thinks, constantly asking him questions that he always answers in a carefully considered way. He says that in the many years since the murder there hasn't been a single day when he hasn't thought about it or woken up in the night dreaming of it. I ask him about remorse.

'I regret that I killed her. Julie and I weren't happy together, but her death wasn't the answer. I regret the pain I've caused, but that relationship was toxic from the start. I can't feel sorry that she is gone, I'll always be relieved.'

This is the account he always gives, which is why his attempts at parole have so far been unsuccessful. After the first few sessions, I realise that Steve has never held eye contact. He is always cleaning, loves order, hates loud noises.

'Have you ever been assessed for autism, Steve? I've looked in your file and there's no mention of it.'

I'm surprised to see that he's never been assessed, and so I arrange it. I don't think that he can lie or play the game. I've spent more time with Steve than his previous officers; this is partly because I have three other clients in the same prison, so often visit them at the same time. He describes events as truthfully as he sees them and discussing feelings just doesn't seem possible for him.

After the assessment, Steve is diagnosed with Autistic Spectrum Disorder, which may go some of the way to explaining why he struggles to verbalise remorse, but it might also explain his actions to *some* degree. Of course, being autistic doesn't mean someone will be violent but Julie managed to push every one of Steve's buttons – getting in his face, being loud, putting the radio on to be louder still – meaning he was not able to process his emotions. Though it wasn't Julie's fault and she didn't deserve to die, the diagnosis provides context for his actions.

I feel almost proud that, despite the difficulties Steve has describing his feelings, he has done his best and shared his trauma. Before becoming a Probation Officer, I wasn't prepared for the detailed, often personal information we hear, and thus how significant our job is. Steve has never spoken to anyone apart from Probation Officers like me, the odd psychologist or passing prison officer. I know that because of this I am one of the only people who can make a thoroughly informed assessment about his suitability for release – I am the only one who noticed his autism. I recognise that if I am good at my job, it will not only be Steve who shares his deepest thoughts and feelings with me, but that many people will tell me things that they have never told anyone before and that I will be making decisions that affect them, the victims and society. I feel both invigorated and nervous.

Three years after first meeting him, I explain in Steve's parole report that due to his autism he is not capable of displaying remorse in the traditional sense. I describe his constant cleaning, his sadness at what he did, the fact that he remembers it every day and propose that these are all indicators of how he feels even if the words elude him. I also say that after many meetings with him I believe that his risk of reoffending is low.

Steve gets parole.

He is adamant he will never drink alcohol again. I regularly test him. There is never a trace. He also says he will never have a relationship again.

Steve regains his liberty as an institutionalised, socially inadequate elderly man. He is always house-proud when I visit him in his perfectly clean flat. In my efforts to engage him in conversation since, I have observed that he only has three interests: cleaning, the local football team and 1970s 'dad rock'. I once made the mistake of telling him that my husband Tom supports the same team as him, which Steve misinterpreted as me being interested.

More engrossing though, are his cleaning tips, which would give Mrs Hinch a run for her money.

Steve still recounts how surprised he'd been at how beautifully the Persil had removed those blood stains from the grouting, and how he had privately admired it before the police came to arrest him. 'I use Aldi own brand now. I couldn't use Persil again after *that*. Of course, there was no Aldi then, I love it. Just as good as Persil and half the price.'

I've adopted Steve's methods at home and can highly recommend the washing powder paste – it's worked wonders on the grease at the back of my cooker for years. I also use cola to wash the floor and a wet flip-flop to get rid of fluff.

Following his release from prison, I realise that telling him my husband supports the same football team has been a mistake. The match is Steve's weekly excursion. Every week he asks where Tom stands and every week Tom is paranoid that he will have to make small talk with a murderer on the terraces. Of course, neither knows what the other looks like nor where they stand, so they have never met – but it doesn't stop either from looking. During our sessions Steve narrates the matches to me in real time and I have trouble keeping myself awake – Tom has already given me a play-by-play and I was bored then. I think instead of what to cook for dinner, as Steve talks to himself.

Steve is the most boring man I've ever met. Though, to be fair to him, in the fifteen years I have worked with him I've been married twice, had children, moved house three times, been on countless holidays, attended weddings and funerals, whereas all he's been able to do is listen to some football on the radio (the team are too crap to be televised), read books and learn how to make an alcohol-based cleaning product out of Marmite. Anyone who says that prison isn't a punishment is wrong.

I see him in the community for some eight years after his release. He lives in a warden-controlled local authority retirement home. The warden knows what he did, but none of the other residents have the faintest idea. The warden informs me that everyone thinks Steve is a bit boring, but they're happy to listen to him talk about his favourite football programmes so long as he puts their bins out and goes to the shops for them. He is *almost* popular and has the quiet, uneventful kind of life that he always craved. He has never given me any cause to believe that he would reoffend. In fact, most murderers do not commit further offences once they are released from prison, despite what the media might imply.

When someone is sentenced to life imprisonment it means that, even after their release, they continue to be on licence until their death. This starts with supervision in the community, a process that lasts until they're deemed to no longer pose a risk to society or themselves. At this point, their Probation Officer applies to the Ministry of Justice for the supervised part of their licence to stop.

***

After a few years on licence, I am convinced that – short of boring someone to death – Steve won't harm anyone, so I apply to the Ministry of Justice to end his supervision in the community. We must talk about the murder again for the inevitable report and Steve states outright that he has never really felt clean following the murder – that's why his flat is stuck in this never-ending spring clean. The legacy of the murder is embedded into his daily routine. It's like he can't shake the split-second decision he made all those years ago as a young man.

I try to check whether any of Julie's family object to his not being supervised anymore, but the offence took place so long ago I can't trace anyone. It pains me that a woman lost her life and that there is nobody around to grieve or advocate for her memory. She will never be able to tell her version of events. As Steve is the only witness, she will always be remembered as being primarily argumentative and loud. Steve's family are also dead and so he is alone with his collection of football programmes and outdated albums. His time in prison abruptly arrested his development; he's stuck in the time before he went away.

'I'll be happy not to have to talk about it anymore, Lizzie. I'll be glad when our supervision is over,' he says at our last meeting.

He never said he missed Julie, only that he was relieved their marriage was over. If he had tried to convince the Parole Board that he was sorry he might have been released a few years earlier. Perhaps to his credit, he felt compelled to maintain a truthful account of his feelings.

It's funny really, having been bored stiff by Steve every few weeks for a number of years, I miss him now. I'll never forget him – I can't fry sausages or look at my grouting without thinking of him.

In our first meeting I said to him that he could tell me anything. All these years later I still say this whenever I meet someone new but now add: 'You can tell me anything. I've heard it all before and you can't shock me.'

I am almost unshockable now and I mostly really have heard it all before.

***

A few years after first meeting Steve, Tom and I start a family. I mostly read files in my kitchen, away from prying eyes. We aren't supposed to take them home, but we're all too busy to read them at work. Like millions of other working mothers around the world, I still do the bulk of the household chores. I know there are some great dads and partners who do more of their fair share than mine does, so I shouldn't make such sweeping generalisations. However, I listen to *Woman's Hour* and all the women say they do more, so it must be true.

Before I go to work, I get the kids up, cook breakfast, put the washing on, clean up, take the dog out, do poo patrol after the dog (and after Tom, who despite being an adult still hasn't worked out how to clean a toilet), and take the kids to school. Then, after an eventful day at work, having listened to people talk about why they stabbed that guy or why it's totally fine to masturbate while fantasising about a six-year-old, I take the washing out, walk the dog, vacuum, cook dinner, clean up, then look bright and breezy as my family regale me with how hard they've worked and exhausted they are, before helping the kids with their homework.

Three times a week I accompany the kids to their various drama clubs, where I sit and look fascinated by their performances and congratulate them on their brilliant acting skills (I am genuinely proud). Tom occasionally empties the dishwasher, after which he will throw me a triumphant look and I must profusely thank him for how well he's put the dishes away and remind him that he's amazing. I tell him that he's not a 'traditional man' at all, as I shoo the children to bed. He then positions himself in the living room and watches war documentaries because he's 'exhausted' after mansplaining that men get more tired than women because of their hard physical labour.

While he's watching television, I read files from work, because there aren't enough hours in the day. Honestly, I'm surprised more murders aren't committed by exhausted mothers desperate for a clean, quiet house. I know I sometimes eye the frying pan with longing.

3

Stella

I was in the house with my friend Jeff. We were having dinner, and we could hear lots of shouting outside. Suddenly, a piece of brick flew through the front window. It only just missed my head; I could have been killed. There was glass everywhere. I was terrified for my life. I ran upstairs where I could peek out of the window and I saw that it was Stella, my ex. She's a nutter. She was screaming in the street that she was going to kill me and waving a knife around. She was shouting that she was going to chop my balls off and stab me. I fully believed that she would break in and do it. I feared for my safety. I immediately called the police, who were there in ten minutes. She spent the entire time outside screaming and shouting. Ten minutes is a long time when you are that afraid.

No, she didn't attempt to get into the house, but she would have if the police hadn't arrived. She wanted to kill me; she's said it before. I believed that she would carry out her threat this time. We split up a couple of months ago. What a relief that was. I've been so much happier since she left. She was a crazy woman.

***

Like so many of my clients, I am first introduced to Stella at my kitchen table. She isn't there in person; I am reading about her, getting ready to write a Pre-Sentence Report for her hearing in the Crown Court.

Stella's file is open in front of me. I look around at the newly decorated room and admire the olive-green walls for a few moments before catching sight of the sink full of washing up and hastily returning to the file. Stella has been charged with Threats to Kill, Possession of an Offensive Weapon, Criminal Damage and a Section 2 Public Order Act. All in relation to her ex, 'Keith'.

Keith's friend Jeff's account is largely the same as his:

> Keith is well rid of her, she was shouting 'you deserve to be dead, I'll cut your fucking balls off'. Keith was really scared, especially when the brick came through the window.

It's difficult not to build an image of a witness or suspect when reading their statements, and, for some reason, I have a sudden picture of Jasper and Horace, the two shady friends from the Disney version of *101 Dalmatians*.

Next comes the statement provided by the neighbour, Agatha, who had watched the whole incident from across the street, forfeiting *Eastenders*; clearly the real-life drama was more entertaining. Judging by her very detailed witness statement, Agatha had enjoyed being interviewed by the police and the whole incident had provided a very engrossing evening.

> I saw it all. Stella was outside Keith's house. She left him a couple of months back, poor man. He's well

rid of her. The police were always here before she left. This is a quiet street. We don't want her sort here. I shut the window in the end, I couldn't stand hearing all that swearing any longer.

Lastly, I read Stella's statement.

> All the times he's beaten me, when he broke my arm, he's broken my ribs. I must have called you twenty times; you've literally never done anything to help me. I've begged you, even the hospital rang you and fuck all. And now this, you arrest me just for shouting outside his house. It's a fucking joke. I'm going 'No comment'.

True to her word, Stella didn't answer another question. She was given bail to appear in court and the court adjourned for her to see me, to find out a bit more and to assess her for an appropriate sentence.

I close Stella's file and try to conjure a picture as I wash up. I've started to build an image of what led to her offence. I expect someone imposing, maybe buxom, confident, tall. I am curious to meet her, as I am with all new clients.

The next day I open the door to the waiting room and am struck by what I see. Stella is a petite, smartly dressed young woman with short hair. Her skin is clear and bright; she wears no make-up, no jewellery. If anything, she looks like an adolescent boy. I call her into the office. She looks frightened. It reminds me of myself all those years ago. I keep things professional, but I want to hug her and tell her that everything will be all right. She seems vulnerable, more typical of a victim, not the hard 'nutter' described in the witness statements. I place a box of tissues on the desk between us. I know we'll need them.

I introduce myself and ask her to sit down.

I explain that this is her opportunity to describe everything that happened from her perspective. 'You've admitted you're guilty, so you have absolutely nothing to lose by talking about it. In my report I can tell the court your side. They haven't heard it yet, but if we can help them to understand your version of events it will help them to make sure you get the right sentence for you.'

Stella immediately starts crying and I nudge the tissues in her direction.

'Don't be kind to me,' she said. 'It always makes me fucking cry.'

Her voice is a little more like I'd imagined, gravelly and deep. It belies her young face. She clearly smokes a *lot*. I brace myself, ready to hear her story.

'Just start from the beginning, Stella. Why don't you tell me about your childhood.'

***

Stella lived with her parents and older brother until she was twelve. Overall, it had been an unremarkable childhood and Stella had been particularly close to her father. She remembers him as a loving, warm, protective presence, constantly looking to find the fun side of things. He was always laughing and there was a real sense of joy in the house. However, he died in a car accident when Stella was just twelve and she was left with her mother who had rarely shown her much affection. In the months following her father's death, her mother turned to drink and fell into violent rages, largely directed at Stella. This eventually led to Stella going into foster care at thirteen, though her brother remained at home.

After Stella turned sixteen, her mother started contacting her again and, elated, Stella moved back home. Her elation was short-lived; soon after moving back, she was raped by her older brother. Her mother failed to believe or protect her, and Stella, despite her youth, was placed in a bedsit. Her brother was never brought to justice and their mother continued to support him. Naturally, Stella is deeply hurt and angered by this, and hasn't spoken to either of them since. She cries as she speaks.

Looking for a father figure, Stella met Keith, fifteen years her senior. Daunted by loneliness and desperate for someone to love her, she quickly moved in with him. Even in the beginning something about the relationship felt wrong. Yet within months they were married. Keith was very strict and set Stella a harsh regime of chores, effectively making her his maid. Given her young age, she had little experience of running a home, but his expectations were high. She learned quickly, but her attempts at being the perfect housewife were never good enough for him. He complained about her cleaning, her cooking, her appearance; in fact, everything. For many years, she was the victim of considerable domestic violence, but nobody ever helped her. During her marriage, she sustained broken ribs, a fractured nose and black eyes. She had been admitted to hospital multiple times, where doctors had raised their concerns with the police, but each time the police came Stella would be too scared to tell them what had happened and would patch together some flimsy tale about being clumsy or falling over and they would leave, taking no further action.

'I could give him as good as I got verbally,' Stella says. 'I used to scream and shout at him to fucking get off me, but it made it so much worse. In the end I just used to sit and take it and wait for him to finish. I didn't call the police anymore either, 'cause the bastards didn't do anything.' Eventually, she plucked up the courage to leave him. While she was relieved, finally safe in her own home, she was also angry. Why should he get to keep their house while she was back in a shabby bedsit?

Just like her brother before him, Keith had hurt and abused her, but no one had cared. He kept the house, his good name intact. And once again Stella was abandoned.

The night of the offence, a switch flicked in her mind. She just *knew* he'd be spending his evening relaxing with his dickhead mate Jeff. She'd had enough and, for the first time in her life, she felt *confident*. Armed with a knife, she genuinely wanted to cut his fucking balls off. She was possessed. Exhilarated as she screamed outside his house, she picked up a brick and hurled it through his window. If nobody was going to help her, she'd have to sort things herself.

Stella looks at me with a twinkle in her eye as she describes that night. I can't help but smile back at her. She explains: 'I carried on shouting at the police too, told them they were fucking bullies. I didn't struggle, but bastard men, they're all the fucking same.'

I understand how she felt. I've heard it so many times before: how women haven't been heard or believed, raped with no follow-up, or victims of domestic violence where the perpetrator hasn't been charged. Of course she felt like screaming. They are victims who take matters into their own hands because they feel they have no choice, but I still think to myself, *You didn't do yourself any favours, Stella.* For the time being though, I stay silent and give her space to consider what she wants to say. Over the years, I've learned that being quiet makes people talk more – they want to fill the void that silence opens – so I give her one of my encouraging nods and she carries on, eventually admitting that she felt really vulnerable. In my head I cheer: result!

I am going to make sure her version of events is in the report as this will provide vital context as to *why* she committed the offence. Sentencing guidelines for 'Threats to Kill' are wide ranging, and therefore Stella might be sentenced to anything from an order served within the community, such as Probation or Community Service, to seven years in custody. Ensuring her perspective is properly recognised can make a huge difference to her eventual sentence. Though my job is to remain impartial, I want to make sure she gets a sentence where I can supervise her in the community and help to rehabilitate and counsel her, both for her own good and to make sure she doesn't break any more of Keith's windows.

On the day of Stella's sentencing, she's perched in the witness box looking small and frightened. The Crown Court is full of posh people – the judge and barristers floating about in their gowns and wigs, plus all the others who work there wearing their best suits. Three weeks prior, the court had adjourned for 'reports', just like they do on the television. This basically means the Pre-Sentence Report. My report. I've written hundreds of them, but I'm nervous too. I'll be recommending what sentence Stella gets and if the judge goes along with my proposal, which they usually do, I can finish my day with the satisfaction of a job well done. On the other hand, he could undermine me in front of Stella, and publicly humiliate me in front of all these people wearing capes.

Having said that, I love working in the Crown Court. A rush of adrenaline floods through me when my Pre-Sentence Report cases are going to be heard. There is drama, the suspense of what's going to happen, but there's also love, both for the worried families of perpetrators and, of course, for the victims. Sometimes you even see the families of victims and perpetrators talking and hugging, the experience of court overwhelming and terrifying for both sides. While it can be traumatic for victims to see perpetrators for the first time since the offence, it can also be cathartic. Facing demons can be an important part of the healing process. You see the full maelstrom of human emotion play out. It's like a play and I'm part of the cast. If you like the theatre and can't afford the tickets, I highly recommend going to sit in the public gallery for the day. Not only can you observe the cases unfold, but during the breaks you can sit in the tearoom and eavesdrop on the barristers talking about what mood the judge is in that day and how they anticipate events will turn.

All cases in the Crown Court sit before a judge, 89.6 per cent of whom are white.* And if you close your eyes just about

---

*   'Ethnicity facts and figures: Judges and tribunal members', Gov. UK, 3 October 2024: https://www.ethnicity-facts-figures.service. gov.uk/workforce-and-business/workforce-diversity/judges-and-non-legal-members-of-courts-and-tribunals-in-the-workforce/latest/.

one hundred per cent sound like a member of the royal family. When I first started working in the Crown Court in the 1990s, barristers were also almost universally white men, though this has gone down to fifty-one per cent. There is a better class spread now too, though most remain privately educated – or at least sound it. Many offenders, on the other hand, have had a very different experience of education. A large proportion of them are unable to read or write: fifty-seven per cent of prisoners have a reading age below that of the average eleven-year-old.* It is noticeable, too, that many offenders had a rough start, born into poverty and deprivation, often with little affection or parental guidance. So it often comes across like posh people coolly deciding the fate of the poor.

There are lots of other people in the middle, however, including the Probation Officers, ushers and admin staff running around doing lots of work with little reward, probably a bit like society at large. However, as a result of very significant cutbacks and changes in legislation by the government, the whole of the criminal justice sector is struggling. Now, *everyone* is doing lots of work with little reward. Even barristers, who used to seem to have it so easy, have been out on strike. Twenty-three per cent of them work more than sixty hours a week and the average salary for the first three years of

---

* 'Prison education: a review of reading education in prisons', HM Inspectorate of Prisons, Ofsted, 22 March 2022: https://www.gov.uk/government/publications/prison-education-a-review-of-reading-education-in-prisons/prison-education-a-review-of-reading-education-in-prisons.

employment was £12,200 in 2022.* Those doing state-funded defence work (legal aid) are the worst off, thereby reinforcing the class divide, as the more experienced are choosing to do more lucrative work, thus leaving those offenders who need decent representation with the less experienced, much more tired and stressed, barristers.

The judge has complete power in court and can belittle anyone with a few curt words if they so choose. Stella's defence gives a speech about her life and offers mitigation about why she committed the offences, to which the judge listens intently for a few minutes before telling them to sit down as he's heard enough, just short of asking him not to waffle on. My report is read by the defence barrister, who was too busy to write their own report, and thankfully, it's not undermined by the judge. I describe Keith as the victim, because he is in the eyes of the law, but I am able to say that 'Stella experienced a difficult relationship with him' and 'I have confirmed with her GP that she has been in hospital a number of times, with broken ribs, nose and various other unexplained injuries', which alludes to him being a bastard. Everyone in court knows exactly what I mean, except Keith, who still thinks he's a good guy.

Since she is eligible to go to prison, I mention that in my view a custodial sentence would do little to change her behaviour and, while it would punish her for the duration, it would introduce her to more sophisticated offenders and thus

---

* Haroon Siddique, 'Junior criminal barristers "despair" over pay deal in England and Wales', *Guardian*, 11 October 2022: https://www.theguardian.com/law/2022/oct/11/junior-barristers-despair-over-pay-deal-in-england-and-wales.

potentially increase her risk of reoffending. More importantly, she has had a life without opportunities and it's time for her to have a chance.

What I really want to say is, 'I know she's been very naughty, but it's not her fault, everyone has let her down. Please oh please don't send her to prison, we can save her, honestly, she's a good egg really, oh go on, your honour, PLEASE!' But unfortunately, you can't speak normally in court. You must stick to court language, so I conclude by declaring, 'In my view a robust community order would reduce her risk', and recommend a Probation Order.

The judge, ultimate arbiter of justice, then sums up. This is usually littered with court speak, which nobody except the people who work there understand. So, once he has risen and departed, everyone has a perplexed look on their faces, wondering what just happened until the barristers, Probation Officers and ushers run around interpreting, and you can see the lights go on in the faces of everyone concerned.

He sees Stella as a victim. She looks at me and gives a half smile – vindicated. It's clear he hasn't missed a single word either from the barrister or my report. Judges' listening skills should never be underestimated; they are forensic in their consideration of the particulars.

Generally, court judges are intuitive and wise, and everyone is shit scared of them. Tom and I were recently walking the dog in the countryside when I spotted an old man in his wellies trudging along with his dog. I almost dropped to my knees in a curtsey, and went bright red. Tom, next to me, was baffled. When the old man said 'Hello, Miss Baxter,' I could hardly believe he knew my name and couldn't stop talking about it for the rest of the day, like I'd met a film star. It was the judge from the local Crown Court. Tom thought I was nuts.

Stella gets an eighteen-month Probation Order. I see her legs buckle in the dock as she weeps with relief before exiting.

Despite working there, I still find the Crown Court a fearsome place. That day is no different to any other for me or the others at work. As usual between cases, there is the hum of chatter between prosecution and defence barristers, solicitors, ushers, all talking about anything but work. Instead, it's what to have for dinner, how the kids are. I'm often conscious of the contrast between the extreme emotions experienced by defendants and victims, and the humdrum stuff of everyday life continuing on for the staff. It feels like there's a total disconnect between the defendants and those who are sitting in judgement on them. Probation offers an important link between the two groups of people, but I do feel conscious that I'm pulled towards the establishment, so desperate am I to be respected by the judge.

I organise Stella's first appointment with me on the steps of the court before charging back inside for my next case, pushing her to the back of my mind until I'm at home later, vacuuming and mentally summing up my day, wondering why nobody else has cooked dinner, before trying to forget work again.

We see all sorts of female offenders in Women's Centres, where no men are allowed in case the domestic violence victims see their partners or prostitutes bump into their clients or pimps in the waiting room. Eighty-five per cent of all crimes are committed by men, and while figures vary year-to-year, on average less than ten per cent of murders are committed by women.* I have worked with several murderers; none of them were women acting alone – the two women I have worked with helped their male partners to kill people. Offending simply isn't viewed as within the spectrum of normal female behaviour, so when they do offend, society tends to come down harder.

Looking after female offenders takes more time and patience and involves a lot more counselling. When you start to dig, many of them, like Stella, are in trouble because their lives were atrocious from the start; they've been abused as children and beaten up by their partners as adults. There are obviously female offenders who are simply criminals, but in my experience, these are very much in the minority.

At Stella's first session after her sentence, we talk strategy. As I see it, building her confidence would be a good start. Due to the turbulence of her teenage years, she never completed her education. On top of that, Keith had told her she was useless so often that she had eventually believed him, and her self-esteem was now on the floor.

Things can't change overnight. Probation Officers can't just tell people to stop offending; it wouldn't work. We tailor supervision sessions to suit each client, and use a variety of methods, including pro-social modelling (setting good

---

* Ninety-three per cent of murders between 2018 and 2020 were committed by men. See Lizzie Dearden, '93% of killers in England and Wales are men, official figures show', *Independent*, 11 March 2021: https://www.independent.co.uk/news/uk/crime/women-murders-men-ons-sarah-everard-b1815779.html.

examples), motivational interviewing (listening and building upon positive statements) and positive reinforcement (everyone loves praise). All these methods can be painfully slow, but they are effective.

These techniques are also surprisingly effective at home. I try not to tell my family what to do directly as I know this causes disharmony – there is rarely shouting or arguing, and I mostly get my own way. In the twenty odd years we've been together I've persuaded Tom to get a dog, buy a house and have children. He still doesn't remember when he officially agreed to these things.

I treat Stella with respect and listen to her (pro-social modelling). She had always said that nobody would employ her, but after an interview at the Women's Centre she was offered work as a volunteer. This really built up her confidence (positive reinforcement). We talk about how she would be happier if she was out volunteering rather than staying in her bedsit alone. For the moment it wouldn't matter if she didn't get paid, it's about being happy (motivational interviewing).

Stella does so well at the Women's Centre they ask if she'd like to volunteer in a public-facing role once a week on reception.

'What, me? Answer phones and shit?'

'You can do it, Stella, especially if you stop swearing!'

'For fuck's sake, all right,' she laughs. She stands up straighter, her demeanour changing before my eyes. She is good on reception. The women like her. They confide in her because she understands them – she's been there too. She enrols on a basic computer skills course and passes.

'I've got a certificate, Lizzie!' she says. 'I've never had one before. I want to do another course.'

That September she enrols at the local college for GCSEs in Maths and English, making new friends along the way. Months later, having gained both some experience on reception and her GCSEs, she applies for a job and gets it. It is her first-ever paid employment. She is delighted.

'I'm nearly as happy as when my dad was alive, Lizzie.'

She makes me feel happy too, like we've achieved something.

One day she tells me she has a boyfriend.

'I think I'm in love.'

I hope that, in view of her newfound confidence, she wouldn't get involved in another unhealthy relationship, but as a precaution I investigate her new boyfriend. I can hardly believe it. Her new love is a man called Ben Jones, a convicted rapist. I want to say to Stella, 'What the fuck are you doing?'

I recall a conversation I'd had with Mick a few days before. He'd been chuntering about one of his clients: 'Bloody Ben Jones says he's in love. Another one we've got to keep a closer eye on.' We decide to work together to keep Stella safe, sharing information. I can't believe her judgement is this bad. Mick makes sure that Ben has an 8 p.m. curfew so he can't stay overnight with Stella. We inform all the relevant agencies about the relationship so we can all keep an eye on her. Somewhat surprisingly, Stella is rather pleased with us intervening and preventing her from spending a full night with her new boyfriend. She says that nobody has ever tried to protect her before, and she likes it. Ben is equally compliant with Mick, telling him how he regrets his offence and how he deserved the time in prison, but that he has changed and is willing to do whatever it takes to be with Stella. She continually talks about how lovely Ben is. Maybe eight years behind bars for rape taught him a lesson... or maybe he is biding his time. None of us are totally sure, but we do everything we can to minimise any risk of harm.

In a way, I'm glad she got arrested. It has meant she now has people looking out for her. She has learnt how to stand up for herself without standing outside someone's house waving a knife around. I'm certain she'll never be arrested again.

At the end of her eighteen months, it's time to say goodbye. Stella is still in her bedsit, but happy and settled. She has a job as a receptionist and has managed not to swear at anyone. She's considering going back to night school.

She has plans for her future. It's her dream to be a social worker one day.

'I really understand what it's like to be on the other end of social services, I think I could do a really good job there,' she tells me.

Sometimes it's difficult to say goodbye, especially when you've seen such change and growth. But, like the others, Stella is a client and not a friend and so, after summing up her eighteen months and telling her how pleased I am for her, we exchange a quick hug, and she is gone from my office.

I see her in the street a few years later. She looks totally different – gone is the boyish look. She's wearing make-up and looks sophisticated. I'm pleased to see her.

'How are you?'

'I'm happy, I've got a house now and guess what? I'm training to be a social worker!'

'Oh my God, Stella! That's amazing. And what happened to the rapist?'

'You can't call him that anymore! He's Ben and yes, we're still together. We got married. I love him.'

She certainly looks happy. I feel bad for calling him the rapist. I should know – people can change.

4

Jake

I'm going on a road trip to see Jake, an arsonist. He's in a prison many miles away from home and the meeting is important as it could determine if and when he can be released. He's one of my Imprisonment for Public Protection (IPP) clients. David Blunkett introduced IPP sentences in 2003 to protect the public from criminals deemed too dangerous to be released once the term of their original sentence had finished. The idea was that they would remain in prison until safe, and until that time there would be facilities and education programmes in prison that would fully rehabilitate them. It sounds like a reasonable idea in theory but in practice it means that there are around 3,000 desperate inmates who don't know when – if ever – they will be free. Even David Blunkett now describes the policy as a 'disaster' and 'immoral', and although Kenneth Clarke scrapped the scheme in 2012, those sentenced under the scheme still don't have a release date.

My job today is to assess Jake and write a report for the Parole Board recommending whether he is safe to be released or should stay in prison.

Initially, I was just going to drive to the prison, interview Jake, then dash home again, but when I told my mum where it was, she suggested that I bring her and my auntie, Jackie, along. There's a pretty town nearby where I could drop them off for the day. I agree, glad to break up my journey.

Later, I call Jake's mum, Jean.

'I'm going to see Jake tomorrow; do you have any messages for him?'

'Oh, you are so lucky to see him. I haven't seen him in over a year, I wish I could go too…'

She sounds so despondent. Without thinking it through I hear myself asking, 'Would you like to come with me?'

'Yes please! I've missed him so much. I just want to see his face. We can't talk properly on the phone. I want to see that he's all right with my own eyes.'

Feeling guilty, I then call my mum to tell her that I can't take her now.

'We were really excited about our day out; why can't you just take us all?'

I can hear the disappointment in her voice and feel even more guilty, but this time in the way that only your mum can make you feel. I suppose she's right; there's no real reason they can't all come. I feel uncomfortable though – while Jean isn't a criminal, it's the first time my personal life has collided with work so transparently.

I give Mum firm instructions: if they are coming, they must not interrogate Jean or ask any questions about Jake. I tell her that Jake is in prison for arson but give no other details. She immediately responds with a rant about criminals and the dangers of fire, proclaiming, 'He deserves to be in prison, he should be there forever, and they should throw away the key.'

Rolling my eyes, I give strict orders to her *not* to express her views in front of Jean. I'm sure she'll change her mind once she's met Jean, but I'm still slightly worried about her voicing her feelings out loud. I also instruct them not to talk about our family or give away any details about us. Then I warn Jean that my mum and auntie will also be in the car and tell her that despite my instructions my mum is unlikely to resist asking some questions or making inappropriate comments. Jean seems unperturbed, grateful for the lift to see her son over a hundred miles away. Jean doesn't drive and the prison is almost inaccessible any other way.

I tell Mick that I'm worried about our trip and how I now wish I was going alone. His helpful contribution to my legitimate concern is, 'Are you taking a picnic and some incontinence pants?'

I do sometimes worry about Mick's understanding of women's biology. My three passengers are in their sixties. But a picnic is a great idea. They can't talk as much if they're eating...

After a year not seeing her son, Jean buzzes with excitement. She even cries at the thought that she will be with him so soon. Her tearful response reminds me that though for me seeing Jake is a job, for her it is her life. Her baby. Her son. His future. I feel the weight of responsibility bearing down on me. I hope I do his assessment justice.

In real terms the IPP sentence means that the length of time Jake serves is determined by his behaviour in prison and the bureaucracy of the Parole Board system. When I look at Jean, I can't help pondering how I would cope if my son were in Jake's place.

Jake is only twenty-seven years old and has been in custody for eight of those. He's a very different person to the teen who went in. The regularity of reviews has been set by the Parole Board, who decided at the last hearing that they wouldn't review the case again for two years.* In view of funding cuts, most of the courses for IPP inmates are no longer available. Completion of courses was one of the prerequisites for release, so without any availability that box can't be ticked, through no fault of the inmate. They know that one of the only things that will determine the likelihood of release is their behaviour in prison, but some find behaving well difficult when there is little hope of release and no date to work towards. They therefore look forward to the parole reviews with fear and trepidation as each one has the fate of their life in their hands.

Personally, I believe that Jake should have been released after the last hearing, which is what I recommended in my report. I'm doing everything possible to help get him released after the upcoming hearing, hence my trip to see him. It's an important visit and I'm unsure if the distraction of my guests will be helpful or not.

My mum has been excited and intrigued to meet a 'real' criminal's mum and looks surprised when Jean gets into the car. She hasn't got a single tattoo on her face, and she's still got teeth. *Clearly* not what Mum had expected. She is

---

* This changed in 2019, allowing an inmate to appeal a decision.

a petite, pretty woman with perfectly applied make-up and immaculate red lipstick. She's had her hair cut for the visit; it's short and dark, accentuating her delicate features. She looks elegant and smart, even though she's only wearing jeans, a white shirt and trainers.

My mum introduces herself in her poshest accent. I look at her pointedly in the mirror and her accent gradually fades back to normal.

I examine my own smart dress. When I chose it this morning, I was conscious that it really needed ironing, but that picnic wasn't going to pack itself. I look a bit dishevelled and suddenly feel ashamed that I haven't made the same effort as Jean.

Jean is a lovely woman but I still feel slightly uncomfortable. This is the nearest I've ever come to allowing one of my clients 'in'. None of them know anything about me, so introducing one to members of my family doesn't sit right. I choose instead to focus on what the day is actually about. I am meeting the prison Probation Officer and Jake's Personal Prison Officer, who should have gathered information about Jake and reached out to others who've worked with him in the prison, like the educational and psychological teams, as well as other prison officers. This information will play a pivotal part in my report. His mum will have the opportunity to have an extended visit with him as she's coming with me. There will be time to really talk to each other and even hug. I'm hoping that this insight into their relationship will provide further information for my assessment.

Our motley crew makes the one hundred mile or so journey, chatting convivially. Jean talks about Jake and my mum and Aunt Jackie talk about our family as I glare into the rear-view mirror, throwing my mum the 'I told you not to say anything about our family' look but, all in all, it's fine. My mum and Jackie have resisted the urge to interrogate Jean and have generally behaved themselves. I drop them off in the local town while I escort a palpably nervous Jean into the prison.

Once we get inside, I am told that the Probation Officer is unable to see me. I am seething. It's bloody typical. It's all too common that prison staff may or may not be available and in turn inmates may or may not agree to see you. Long journeys to the other side of the country can be a complete waste of time and, to add insult to injury, you never get offered any tea or coffee for your trouble, just get told to visit again when it's more convenient (for them). Poor Jean looks crestfallen. We are told to come back later in the afternoon as the meeting with the Personal Officer can still go ahead. We leave the prison, meet Mum and have some lunch before heading back. Jean is thoughtful and quiet; I can see that she is as upset as I am irritated.

Prison visits rarely take more than two hours, and we aren't allowed to take our phones in with us, so I tell Mum that I'll call her when we're out to arrange to meet up again. In the event, the Personal Officer isn't available either, so in terms of my report the visit is a total waste of time. Feeling angry, I hope that we independently agree with each other when they present their reports to the Parole Board and that there is no surprise information at the hearing that will make my assessment worthless.

However, I do get to spend more time with Jean and Jake together and it's lovely to behold. They hug and cry.

JAKE

We all talk together; he's made some profound changes. He says he's played by the prison rules and done everything asked of him and more. He works in the prison garden and I meet his boss there, who clearly thinks Jake is great. At least I can get information from someone. From what I can see he is more than ready to be released. He is currently in a Category B prison (high security) and will be expected to gradually go through Category C and Category D (open prison) before he can even be considered for release. I wonder how anyone can justify the convoluted bureaucracy of it all. At the last hearing they said that though he wouldn't be released he would be re-categorised to a lower security prison, but that was two years ago and he's still in the same place. This man's youth is pretty much over before it has begun and every day spent in prison embeds the institution into his very soul.

Despite being unable to see the Personal Officer, the prison is slow to let us out and after the visit we are forced to wait a further hour before being released. When we eventually get out and I check my phone I see that I have several missed calls from strange numbers; I listen to the answering machine and there's a message from a strange man, accusing me of abandoning my elderly mother and aunt.

My mum is a massive worrier and given that we were nearly an hour and a half later than expected, she had been beside herself with concern and convinced that Jean and I were being held hostage in prison. She is not one for mobile phones; she had borrowed my dad's but couldn't figure out how to use it, so had been accosting strangers in the street requesting tech support.

There is a further message from a different man helpfully providing a postcode pinpointing my mum and Jackie's exact whereabouts. I wonder why they've provided coordinates for a house on a residential street with no apparent facilities. When we arrive at said destination, my mum and auntie run out of a vicarage. Apparently, in a panic, mum and Auntie Jackie had gotten lost and Mum, who never goes to church, decided that they should go in (a) to seek help and (b) to see if it had a loo. Once they had located the vicar, my mum couldn't help herself – she started telling him all about the hostage situation I was in. Confronted by a pair of cold, anxious middle-aged women, the vicar clearly felt he had little choice but to invite them in, provide them with toilet facilities, counselling and coffee. So they've spent the last hour having a jolly chat with the vicar and his wife.

The pair get into the car, relieved and refreshed after their little adventure, and my mum admits, without a trace of shame, that she was just as worried about how they were going to get home as she was about my safety. She is under the illusion that I'm able to look after myself.

'I didn't even think about getting home,' says Jackie, looking pleased with herself for having scored a caring point above Mum. 'I was just worried about you; I could imagine you in a prison cell with a convict, their hands around your throat, while you were gasping for air and pleading for your life.'

I take a furtive look at Jean to see how she might respond to this crude accusation about prisoners, but I can see that she is lost in thoughts about her son.

On the journey back, Jean is so delighted about having seen Jake that she happily recounts the details of the reunion.

Mum, emboldened by the afternoon's activities and the fact that she is now headed safely home, goes completely against my explicit orders and asks about Jake's offences. I give her the 'shut up' look in the rear-view mirror, which, again, she completely ignores.

Jean starts to tell the story that I've heard many times now. 'Well, really it began when I was a little girl.'

In her characteristic, matter-of-fact way, Jean describes how her father used to hit her mother and that, from a young age, Jean would stand in front of her and try to protect her. Soon the violence was directed at Jean. Any misdemeanour would mean the belt for her, and verbal and physical abuse for her mother. Jean spent her whole childhood on edge, terrified of her father's rages. He was vile and nasty, continually demeaning her in ways that she still finds hard to admit. Jean described how as she got older, there was nowhere she or her mother could go to seek help. Her father was a police officer and local councillor – an influential figure in the community, perceived as being beyond reproach. Who on earth would believe them?

His attitude towards her didn't improve much when she left home at the earliest opportunity, despite the guilt she felt about leaving her mum. Though the physical violence stopped, he took every opportunity to put her down. Jean would have severed contact had it not been for trying to ensure her mother's safety. Frustratingly, Jean's mother refused to leave her father, figuring that while he was in his shed with his beloved model train set, she would have some peace and quiet.

But once Jean had Jake, her father totally changed. He adored his young grandson and Jean felt that she had finally done something right. When Jean's mother died, they visited her father regularly and he appeared the model grandfather, playing with Jake and caring for him, cutting fingernails and changing nappies without complaint. Jean was happy. She felt that she finally had the father she'd always dreamed of. Jake loved him and Jean now trusted her father, so Jake would sometimes spend the night with his granddad.

When Jake was about twelve years old, his behaviour began to deteriorate. He started shoplifting. He got into fights at school. He refused to talk to Jean and therefore Jean, a single parent, enlisted the help of her dad. Jake would stay there overnight more regularly. He told his mum that he didn't want to go, but Jean thought that having a positive male role model would help him.

Nevertheless, Jean and Jake remained very close, even as Jake's behaviour became increasingly challenging. One day, aged about sixteen, Jake told Jean that he didn't want to stay with his grandfather anymore and flatly refused to spend another night there. They continued to visit regularly and it seemed to Jean as though the relationship between her father and her son remained positive. She thought Jake was simply an embarrassed teenager who didn't want to spend a couple of nights each week with his grandfather.

Then, when Jake was eighteen, he returned from an evening at the pub with a group of friends, drunk and in a rage. Charging around the house, he confessed that his grandfather had been sexually abusing him since he was twelve and had only stopped once Jake refused to stay with him anymore.

After much deliberation, Jean and Jake decided to report the abuse. However, the Crown Prosecution Service felt there wasn't enough evidence to take the complaint further. Jake's grandfather rounded on Jean, screaming at her, calling her stupid, a liar, a useless slut and then slapped her, hard, across the face. Jake, frozen, did not intervene.

Later that day, Jake walked to his grandfather's house and waited, unseen across the road, until his grandfather left. He was furious. His grandfather had hurt both him and his mother but had faced no consequences. He snuck around the back of the house into the garden. Peering into the shed, he saw it – his grandfather's model railway. It was his grandfather's pride and joy and had taken years to build. Silently stuffing newspapers and fire lighters under the train set, he set it ablaze, watching as the shed was overcome by flames.

Jake was charged with arson and sentenced to the IPP. Jean felt entirely responsible. In her mind she had failed to protect Jake both from the abuse and then the courts.

Silence falls over the car for a while, as Mum and Jackie digest Jean's story. As predicted, Mum flips from thinking Jake should be locked up forever to concluding that he was a hero who should have set fire to the shed with his grandfather *inside*. Soon the trio are chortling among themselves. I allow myself to enjoy this warm solidarity between three women who have experienced such different lives, but who all intuitively understand one another as mothers. They soon drift off to sleep, certain of a day well spent.

I drive on. The same sadness creeps over me every time I hear Jean and Jake's story. In the eight years Jake has been in prison more details have emerged about his grandfather. We didn't get this information officially, and both Jean and I first heard about it in the local press, but it has emerged that he was a serial abuser and is suspected of raping other young men. Inadequate police investigations, a lack of shared information across agencies, coupled with his standing in the community, meant that he was given free rein for years. I was, and am, sickened by it, and determined to gain at least some justice for Jake and Jean.

I glance in the rear-view mirror at my sleeping mum, probably dreaming about the placard she'll be holding outside the prison begging for the release of all IPP prisoners. Jean and Jackie are also asleep, their mouths slightly open and heads tilted back, gently rolling with the motion of the car.

I struggle to breathe as I realise the faith Jean has put in me.

My day had been a disaster. I'd tried to get information from everyone else who works with Jake, without success. He has one previous caution for assault, but no other record of violence. Despite many requests for information about the caution from the police over the eight years of Jake's sentence so far, I am yet to receive any. I therefore must rely entirely on Jake's account about one violent incident he was involved in. I just hope it's not overly prejudicial in the long run. According to him, he was involved in a fight where nobody was injured. I hope he's telling me the truth. Apart from two other previous convictions for shoplifting, I can't see anything that causes me to believe he shouldn't be released.

JAKE

Just as Jean has put her faith in me, I've had to put my faith in Jake not to lie to me, since I've been unable to get details from anyone else. I drive home worrying about the impending parole report and hearing; a terrifying experience at the best of times. The hearing is set to be held in a month's time.*

***

The parole board turned him down again and by the time I left my job he was still in prison.

---

* Probation officers are now only able to provide their professional opinion rather than to make a formal recommendation with regard to parole.

5

Adam

Thirteen-year-old Adam is tall for his age and stick thin. A skinhead with the face of a cherub. If he'd let his hair grow, it would be a soft, pale blonde. Currently lying face down on the floor, his cheeks are red as he gasps for air but he's still managing to shout, 'Fucking get off!' He wriggles furiously, his scrawny legs kicking out wildly behind him. Sitting on top of him in an effort to keep Adam still is a burly man, dark haired and bearded. He is holding Adam's arms tightly behind his back. The more Adam kicks, the tighter the grip around his wrists, which are turning red and raw. Burly man repeats, 'Calm down!' Adam sounds angry but looks scared. Amid the group of people nearby is a woman looking up at the sky while someone presses tissues to her nostrils, soaking up the stream of blood. The little group are huddled together, united. They look from the bloodied nose to Adam on the floor and back again.

'Are you going to calm down, Adam?'

'No! Are you going to fucking get off me?'

At twenty-nine years old, I'm a mature student, studying to be a Probation Officer, which means training to be a social worker first. I've just arrived on my first day placement at a children's home. I've never met anyone here before so I stand in respectful silence next to the staff and wonder if they would notice if I slipped away. I have the feeling that merely by standing next to them, I've picked a side.

I've never seen anyone be restrained before. It's brutal. Adam is kicking and screaming to be released, but it isn't happening. I'm not sure what to do and feel awkward standing there like a spare part. I didn't particularly mean to pick a side and clearly nobody is in the mood for pleasantries, so I walk over to Adam, kneel on the floor and put my face next to his about to ask if he's all right. He makes a loud gurgling sound from the back of his mouth and shoots a thick green blob of spit. It's supposed to land on me, but in view of his face being pressed against the floor it drips down his own face. I take a tissue from my pocket and wipe it off before asking if he's okay.

'Of course I'm not okay, I've got spit on my face, a fat bastard on my back and now you want a chat.' I start to laugh, always my natural response at the most inappropriate times. Thankfully, Adam breaks into a smile and stops thrashing. Laughter has diffused his rage. The burly man gets off and leads Adam away into the garden, keeping a firm hold on his arm, with me trailing behind.

'Are you just going to follow me around?'

'I don't know anyone else,' I reply.

That first meeting with Adam was the start of a long rapport. And taught me the merits of fully knowing your client's history; a privilege not afforded to most Probation Officers, who no longer have the benefit of social work training or access to the records that really describe the background of those who have been in the care system.

Adam and his two siblings have been in care for over a year. His brothers were both placed in a foster home but Adam, too volatile to find a placement, has been stuck in a children's home. He regularly flies into rages and attacks members of staff, most recently his key worker. Adam says that it was because she was 'pointing' at him and asking him 'stupid' questions but never expanded upon what these questions were. The children's home manager announces that I can be the key worker now. It seems reckless given I've only just arrived, but given the paltry wage paid to children's home staff, the others don't have much more experience than I do. Turnover of staff is endemic, the result of an average pay just a whisker above minimum wage for looking after the most vulnerable children in society. So I understand perfectly why they'd give Adam to someone who is working there for free. Plus, I've already been training for six months, so in comparison to some of the staff with their lack of training I'm practically an old hand.

Adam and his siblings were placed in care after being abused by their father. He would routinely tie them to the radiator and turn it on full, not letting them get away until they begged for his mercy. Adam's siblings would quickly do as they were told, but Adam would grit his teeth and stare his father out, letting the hot metal burn his back. He refused to relent. His back is now covered in scars, testament to both the abuse and his dogged determination. Both parents were eventually given custodial sentences for their cruelty and neglect, leaving the children in the hands of the state.

Adam is completely traumatised. He doesn't trust anyone. His parents, the very people entrusted with his safety and wellbeing, abused his trust in unimaginable ways. He is *very* angry. He hates everyone, but underneath this hatred is fear. His furious outbursts and difficult behaviour lead to regular restraining. The job of the children's home staff is to try to stabilise him enough to go into a foster placement where he can finally experience some prolonged security, maybe even love. My placement is for six months. Not long to help him turn around an entire childhood of trauma, particularly as other people have been trying for a year already, so I set more achievable goals: I don't want him to hit me and I don't want him to be restrained anymore. Witnessing that just once was more than enough for me.

So I avoid asking closed questions. That's what got the last key worker a punch in the nose. Over the next few months of working with him I learn how to handle him. 'What would you like to do today?' I ask, ensuring he is aware of the boundaries. We can go shopping but he also knows exactly how much we can spend. On another occasion he is excited that we can go to the local zoo, but he knows how long we can stay and what he is and isn't allowed to do.

Mostly I listen. I don't fill the silences. I let him have space to speak, in his own time. It's not all plain sailing. Adam has outbursts and throws chairs around the office while I stand in the corner hoping one doesn't hit me. He carries on having tantrums and creating chaos in the children's home. He gets into noisy strops in shops, where I cringe with embarrassment and want to tell irritated passers-by that he's not mine. He can't go to mainstream school because he has hit teachers in the past and thrown chairs, so instead he goes to a pupil referral unit, where he emerges as the most traumatised in a school full of traumatised children.

I manage to persuade the burly man, Rob, not to restrain Adam anymore and instead, he gives him a 'firm hug' whenever Adam starts kicking off. I see glimmers of Adam relaxing, almost sinking into Rob's arms. Adam lets me stroke his head; the stubble feels like suede under my fingers. Eventually, he goes so far as to ask me to stroke it and he stands still and closes his eyes like a cat; these feel like both small and significant steps forward. Adam has only ever been hurt, punished or restrained. One day, after Adam has asked 'Will you stroke my head?', he admits that he's going to carry on kicking off. 'I never want to go to foster care, it's all right here, they won't send me to a family if I keep behaving like this.' He finally feels safe.

He eventually divulges why he would always stare his father out even as the heat bit into his back: 'While I was burning, it meant he wasn't doing anything to my brothers.' He loves his brothers and wants nothing more than to protect them. He's pleased that they are now in mainstream school and happy in their foster placement. Adam seems to have the view that his life should always be less settled than theirs. That somehow by remaining in the children's home and being the naughty one, they are protected. Adam is difficult and volatile, but also loveable and bright with a keen sense of humour and a broad smile. While I am constantly on my guard for flying chairs and temper tantrums, Adam never does hit me and I become very fond of him. A firm bond is also developing between Adam and Rob, and they spend a lot of time play-wrestling with each other, Adam learning that not everyone is going to hurt him. I feel sad and guilty about leaving him at the end of my six-month placement and I'm acutely aware of the temporary nature of relationships for those in children's homes, with high turnovers of staff, and no permanence, their feelings of worthlessness constantly reinforced.

***

Five years later, I am a fully qualified Probation Officer, and Adam is eighteen and in court. It's almost inevitable – the toxic mix of unresolved trauma, anger and alcohol have created someone who likes fighting. I've asked to work with him again. 'Will you stroke my head, Lizzie?' he asks when we meet again. He's still a little boy underneath and I admit I'm pleased to see him again. He hasn't changed much, he's still tall and lanky and sporting a skinhead. He wants to look tough, but it's impossible. I give his head a pat.

'Well, what happened then?'

'He was staring at me "wrong" so I had to hit him.'

'How can you stare at somebody wrong?'

Adam smiles. 'Well, you know what I'm like. I just lost it.'

He is made the subject of a Community Payback Order, basically working for free removing graffiti or digging public gardens. I feel certain I'll be seeing him again though. Sure enough, alcohol leads him to drugs. He says that it helps to block out the memories, but in turn that makes him even more aggressive. He's always spoiling for a fight but the fights become more and more violent until eventually he injures someone really badly. In light of his previous spells in prison, like Jake, he is sentenced to an IPP – Imprisonment for Public Protection – which, at the time, was an indefinite sentence. Adam doesn't appear to mind. After years in a children's home, followed by time in prison, he is so institutionalised that he feels most secure within prison's rigid structure and admits he's made an effort to go back there. He heads off to prison smiling and saying that he's pleased he's been saved from murdering someone. He's now twenty-nine, the same age I was when I first met him, and ready to face a few years in jail.

There is little change to his behaviour inside. He regularly trashes his cell and threatens prison staff. At one point he hits a prison officer and is transferred to the high-security wing of a high-security prison. There is no furniture for him to trash in his cell there, just a mattress on concrete, so he embarks on regular dirty protests, wiping his own excrement on the walls of his cell, untameable. My visits to him – a three-hour train-ride away – are not as regular as I would like, but when I go, he still has the same smile and requests a head stroke. He tells me that I'm the most consistent person he's had in his life. His siblings no longer visit him. It's a tragedy that someone who only spent six months with him in care, and now only sees him because he's in prison, is viewed as a constant. I can still remember the vulnerable boy he once was while everyone else can only see the violent and deranged man he has become.

I'm off to see him today – he's been on one of his many 'dirty protests' and has said he'll only stop if he can see his Probation Officer. I'm pleased to go as I've been worried about him. He's in a well-known prison with a reputation for violence and mutilation among inmates – luckily, Adam has steered clear of this... for now. When I told Tom about the prison's reputation, he said that I had nothing to fear if I was mutilated just so long as they target my jowls, which would save a lot of money on a facelift in the long run. He's always very helpful like that.

I usually try to go to prison in the morning when legal visits tend to take place, with general visiting hours later. But the distance means I'll only make it in the afternoon this time. Standing in the queue with the other prisoners' families, I feel very conspicuous with my briefcase and flat shoes. I'm surrounded by heavily made-up women wearing impossibly high stilettos and lengthy false eyelashes. They are accompanied by men in hoodies and jeans that hang loosely around their hips revealing stretchy grey pants pulled up high. I spot a woman with long grey hair tied into a bun, in minimal make-up and dressed in sensible outdoor clothing. She's clearly a Probation Officer or social worker. The big giveaway is her footwear – purple Doc Martens. We make eye contact and smile, recognising a kindred spirit, and indeed I see her again on her way to one of the wings. I tried to get rid of my Probation Officer markers a few years back after looking in the mirror to find myself staring at a middle-aged parody of a social worker, with dangly earrings, the ubiquitous purple Doc Martens and scraggy hair; I had my hair cut and unceremoniously consigned the dangly earrings and Docs to my local charity shop, to my instant regret.

All the visitors are herded into the prison like sheep, asked to take off our shoes, watches, belts and jewellery before being searched and sniffed by dogs. The prison smells of dog, sweat and disinfectant. Incidentally, this is in complete contrast to women's prisons, which smell of hairspray and toiletries.* It takes nearly an hour just to get inside.

Some prisons have dedicated legal-visit centres, while some of the older ones, like this one, have an interview room on the wing. This prison has cells up and down a long corridor with the interview room at the end and it is there that I wait for Adam. I can look through the open door and see the inmates traversing in and out of each other's cells and onto the wing, going about their daily business. It's noisy with chatter, but the atmosphere is calm. One door has remained locked. After a while, prison officers arrive with a hose pipe and open it, water jetting into the cell, and I recognise Adam's voice shouting 'Fuck off!' One of the prison officers retorts, 'You can't see your Probation Officer covered in shit.' The prison officer then looks over to me and mouths 'Five minutes?' with a thumbs up sign. I return the gesture. The corridor grows louder with the sounds of inmates talking. I'm listening but trying to look nonchalant.

Suddenly, I hear screaming, the guttural sound of someone in agony. Pandemonium ensues. The hose comes out of Adam's cell and the door is quickly locked. I can hear Adam's shouts of 'Let me out!' Prison officers are blowing whistles and barking orders through their walkie talkies; a sense of urgency pushes inmates back into their cells. There is the deafening sound of cell doors locking with both inmates and staff shouting. Something big has just happened, I have no idea what, so I stand at the entrance to the interview room

---

* Apart from Holloway, which had additional notes of mould and rat droppings.

straining to see. Many more members of the prison staff arrive, keys jangling noisily. There also appears to be what looks like a medical team, with a stretcher. It's all very exciting and I crane my neck to see as much as possible, just like the prisoners are doing, their faces pressed against the tiny slots in their cell doors.

Eventually the prison staff and medical team re-emerge from the cell, carrying a stretcher upon which a man lies resplendent in a frilly pink top and skirt. The skirt is dripping with blood. He is screaming in agony. There is a loud rhythmic banging on cell doors as he passes by, the other inmates cheering and clapping. Through the screaming, the man on the stretcher has a moment of clarity and shouts 'I did it!' before being taken off the wing. The din continues as inmates try to converse with each other through the cell doors.

I sit in the interview room, locked on the wing for a very long time before being told that in view of the situation I am unable to see Adam and must be escorted out. I'm desperate to know what has happened. A guard tells me that the inmate in pink is transgender and has been asking for treatment to medically transition for many years. They have finally taken matters into their own hands and tried to cut their own bollocks off with a razor, but things didn't quite go to plan. No more visits were allowed that day and it turned out to be a wasted trip.

To get over the ordeal, I explore the local town before sitting in the church, finding a sense of peace there. I allow myself some time to think about Adam. His life has been dominated by chaos, as a teenager and now adult, mostly instigated by him, but hindsight makes very clear how improbable it would have been for him to break the cycle. Prison isn't the place for him, but there isn't anywhere else for him to go.

On the train home, I overhear a couple discussing the logistics of keeping their affair secret. As a paid-up nosy person, it's great. I am totally enthralled. They are discussing using different phones, who to follow or unfollow on social media, towns to meet in where they won't be caught. They look very respectable, but I am shocked by how skilfully dishonest they are and I wonder if lying is central to living. They sound exactly like criminals discussing their next job. I am most disappointed when they get off the train, leaving me with nothing to listen to.

I try a bit of mindfulness as that's supposed to be good for stressed out people, but my brain is too exhausted to comply, so I start writing up notes from the day, though there is little to report since the visit was aborted. We've just passed a train with Serco written on the side. They are a private company who own some prisons – what's that got to do with trains? I believe they can also provide you with a smear test; I wonder who decided to go from prisons to trains to vaginas. I stare out of the window; it's a long journey and I can't wait to get home. I love being home with my family, not like those poor bastards in prison, who all too often either don't have a home to return to, or if they do it's not usually a place to unwind.

***

Two weeks later, I'm off to see Adam again to interview him properly regarding his next parole hearing, which will be in a month. Mercifully, there are no hiccups this time. He didn't even need to be hosed down first. He has elected not to have an oral hearing, where we all sit around a table together and discuss him – I secretly thank the Lord as they are a terrifying ordeal – so basically this is going to be a paper shuffling exercise and not the full parole hearing I'd expected. It's a joint interview with his Personal Prison Officer. We try to engage Adam about sentence plans, but he's a difficult man. He shuffles about in his chair not listening, so when we ask questions, he doesn't know what we've asked.

If Adam played the game, things would be easier for him, but he steadfastly refuses to. Instead of talking about sentence plans he tells the prison officer about me rubbing his head, which sounds totally inappropriate, and now we are both awkward, as I explain that I've known Adam since he was thirteen. The prison officer appears bored. We both chat with Adam about programmes that are available in the prison such as education and training, but he has refused to try them before and still won't budge. He has been offered counselling within the prison, which he would clearly benefit from, but he won't take it. Any suggestion is met with a defiant look and a refusal to engage. I'd love for him to be transferred to a prison-based secure therapeutic community, but those spots are like gold dust and Adam has said no, so it's pointless even suggesting it. He won't even promise to reduce his dirty protests. When it comes up, he smiles and says, 'I like being hosed down.' He's playing with us, and I feel frustrated about his lack of desire to help himself. The prison officer remains calm throughout the interview, but I notice the pulse in his temples, his face gradually going pink, then purple, until he eventually looks like a plum with burning ears.

We come out of the interview with the prison officer mumbling 'fucking idiot' under his breath. He doesn't know the young, traumatised but likeable Adam that I first met. The Adam who could have been so different had he only experienced love and stability. The prison officer can only think of Adam as he is now. Maybe I wouldn't want to help him either if I had only experienced Adam's taunts or had to hose him down when he was covered in his own shit. But I still feel desperately sorry for him. I'm also furious about his lack of engagement with anything which would make his own life a little better. He has been so deeply emotionally damaged that he is unable to stop self-sabotaging.

I'll make my recommendations in writing about the therapeutic prison, knowing they'll be laughed at because there aren't the resources to provide the care he needs and there is a long waiting list of people who really do want help. There are just sixteen male therapeutic communities within prisons in the UK, all of which have a waiting list. Then my report will be filed away until next time there's a hearing, in two years. At that point his sentence will have come to an end; however, because he's an IPP prisoner, it's unlikely he'll be released unless he has a complete personality change.

IPP sentences throw up a huge moral dilemma and, while thankfully they no longer exist, those like Adam are still subject to the sentence. Adam was originally sentenced with guidance of a three-year term. Had that been an ordinary sentence, he would have been released after eighteen months on parole. He would have had targets and goals to aim for, so he might have engaged with the services offered to him inside that provide hope and reduce risk. Instead, I am convinced that, without a set plan, Adam is refusing to engage and gradually becoming more dangerous as a result. He wants to remain in prison because he feels safe there and is using his IPP sentence to his advantage by actively being disobedient. At the three-year point, the Parole Board are likely to refuse to release him because he hasn't engaged in any courses, and he's been very disruptive. In a normal sentence he would have been released automatically.

And in the unlikely event he is released after three years, with a quick nod from my line manager, I can have him sent back to prison not only if he reoffends but also if I *think* he might. With no evidence, I could have him sent back indefinitely on a baseless hunch. Or maybe because I'm overworked and in a bad mood… Nobody I've spoken to has admitted to doing this but there are rumours.

No trial, no courts, no solicitors. IPP prisoners on licence are haunted by a feeling of impermanence; it's hard to feel settled if you know that you can be recalled to prison so easily and this impacts relationships, employment, accommodation and mental health. The responsibility also weighs heavy on the Probation Officer. Recalls often occur because Probation Officers are so nervous that someone *might* reoffend. That is simply too much power and responsibility for one person to hold. Even though recalls *should* be double-checked by management, some inevitably fall through the net because of lack of staff or are simply ticked off without proper examination.

So, this sentence will be hanging over his head forever. If he is released on an IPP he will face a life of uncertainty. At least in prison, he knows to expect the chaos, the hose, the restraints. There is comfort in this familiarity – even the cell door being locked each night provides a kind of safety. I can fully understand if they decide that he shouldn't be released; nobody knows what damage he will be capable of in the community, not even Adam. But maybe if he didn't feel so hopeless he would behave better. It's impossible to know. Sadly, I'm so busy that it's unlikely I'll be visiting him again for at least another year, so I can avoid thinking about his parole for a few months, but given the gravity of the decisions around parole it is frustrating that I don't have more time to visit regularly. This makes a mockery of our supposedly 'consistent relationship'.

Poor Adam had the worst possible start in life; if the state had invested in his wellbeing and dealt with his trauma properly in the first place instead of putting him in a children's home with poorly trained staff on £13 an hour and students with no experience, he might have had some genuine support and it might have saved the people he has beaten up from harm and him from becoming the man he is now. Even from a financial perspective it would have been better for him to have proper therapeutic intervention when he was thirteen. It costs an average of £53,801 per year to keep someone in prison[*] but an average of just £80 per hour to see an expert trauma counsellor. It might have taken twenty or even thirty sessions, but a strategy of proper care might have changed the trajectory of his life and, in the long run, it would have been a bargain.

---

[*] 'Costs per place and costs per prisoner by individual prison', *HM Prison & Probation Service Annual Report and Accounts 2023–24 Management Information Addendum*, Ministry of Justice, 3 April 2025: https://assets.publishing.service.gov.uk/media/67e51acfba11d0060f606d68/costs-per-place-costs-per-prisoner-2023-2024-summary.pdf.

6

Chantelle

Chantelle thinks this might be the greatest day of her life. She knows she isn't a stunner but she's wearing her best dress and feels fabulous. Sure, the dress might be a little tight, but then she hasn't needed a best dress for years. She's forty-five but a difficult life has made her look older. Her dark hair is pulled back tightly and when she opens her mouth it reveals tombstone teeth. But she has finally taken control of the situation and has never felt so liberated – today she feels beautiful.

    She's standing in a school courtyard, waving her arms above her head. Sitting either side of her are the massive speakers she borrowed from a friend, blasting out the sound of her own voice, which sounds great. Chantelle is a better singer than she thought. She wrote the song for her daughter and she is getting exactly the reaction she had hoped for. She can make out the faces of smiling school children pressed against classroom windows, all singing along. Annoyed teachers circle in the background ordering them back to their seats but the children are hooked and Chantelle is buzzing. Elated, she sings along to the recording: 'They're cunts and they know they are, they're cunts and they know they are, but the biggest cunt of all is Millie Jackson!'

Her daughter, Jade, has been bullied by Millie for months and despite numerous complaints to the school, nobody has listened. Any mother would have done the same. Wouldn't they?

The glorious sound of the children still singing her song lingers in the distance even as she is driven away by the police. Job done. Surely the school will oblige this time? But as she's booked in at the police station and she's telling the custody sergeant why she did it, he stares at her blankly. Chantelle slowly realises that she's done it again – fucked it all up – and Millie isn't going to stop bullying her Jade.

***

Chantelle has been the subject of a Probation Order many times, usually for minor offences involving shouting and causing a commotion in public. She has a string of previous convictions under the Section 5 Public Order Act and this is going to be another. The trouble is, this time the offence was committed at a school, so she has been allocated a social worker. Chantelle is spiralling – what if social services try to take away her children? She lives for her children and can't imagine life without them. She has already received an unsettling visit from a keen, newly qualified social worker. Chantelle was only trying to help Jade, but now realises she's probably made matters worse – Jade is refusing to speak to her, and now she might be taken away.

Chantelle and her family live in a very modest rented house. You can tell it is in a deprived area because it's got a garish, council-sponsored mural splashed across the side. Obviously, someone thought the mural would cheer things up. Like ugly art could compensate for a lack of, say, food. If it were a Banksy, the wall would be worth more than the house, but this particular artwork isn't getting auctioned off anytime soon. There are only two bedrooms so Chantelle's teenage daughters and young son are squashed into bunkbeds and a blow-up bed. I'm there now and frankly, it's a mess, a clear reflection of her chaotic life. Her social worker (who looks about fifteen and probably lives at home with a mum who still makes his bed) has already threatened to have her children taken into care if she doesn't tidy up. In his defence, social workers tend to be named and shamed if they make a cock-up, so I don't blame him for being cautious. However, I hope Chantelle will be given another opportunity to clean up her act before further action is taken.

Chantelle's house is shockingly untidy – even worse than mine. A musty smell hangs about both place and people. Black smudges mar the skin around her 'sovs' (sovereign rings) and a thick fake gold necklace rests on her voluptuous cleavage. Her husband, Clive, whose greasy fingers look as though he has been working under a car, hasn't done a day's work in over ten years. I offer to go round the house with my marigolds. It's a surprisingly satisfying day. Talking with people is great but getting stuck in and doing something that will deliver results in real time feels immediately gratifying. With Chantelle's permission I have enlisted the help of a probation volunteer to assist. In the clipped tone of sergeant majors, we order the family to work. Between us, we transform the house into something more recognisably liveable.

Both Chantelle and Clive get stuck in, enlisting the help of the children. The family work together as a team and there is clearly a strong bond between them. Sure, at first glance, they seem a bit dysfunctional, dealing with problems in unorthodox ways such as singing obscenities to a school full of children. They have a messy house and don't take care of themselves. However, the home is full of love. The children absolutely adore their parents. There is an endearing silliness and warmth in the air. Chantelle and Clive may not look after their children in a totally socially acceptable or 'normal' way, but it feels like a happy home regardless. This contrasts with so many others I see where there is constant conflict and no affection. It feels to me that this family is worth doing some extra work with. It seems to be, despite evidence of domestic neglect, that taking the children away would not serve any of them well. I feel it would be better to support the parents, encouraging them to raise their children a little more thoughtfully. Their eldest daughter is very bright and could benefit from mental stimulation outside of school but taking her away from her family is not the answer. I'm hoping that I can persuade the social worker to put together a package of intervention that will help the family rather than riding roughshod over them and removing the children. My main tactic: talk to the social worker like I'm his mother until he does as he's told.

Chantelle isn't the brightest spark and she and her husband both struggle to communicate verbally. I'm sure her solicitor will be using the phrase 'she lacks the mental capacity' as mitigation for her court hearing. They mumble and slur when they speak, as though intoxicated. They're not. The couple are obviously used to nobody understanding them as they translate for each other and get the children to help too. Maybe Chantelle felt singing through loudspeakers was the only way she would ever be heard.

Monday rolls around and Chantelle is due in Magistrates' Court. Things have been looking up – she and her husband have managed to maintain an *almost* tidy house, the children have been going to school and, while they are still receiving visits from the social worker, there are no care proceedings currently planned. I've primed Chantelle about dressing in a respectful, modest manner and that she should only speak when she is invited to. I have recommended that she should be given Community Service and I'm hoping that the bench will go with it. She is already on a Probation Order for the last time she was out shouting in the street, so any additional supervision would be superfluous.

Before the court goes into session, I spot Chantelle in the waiting room. I am horrified. Her naturally dark hair has been dyed nicotine blonde, her skin stained bright orange and streaked with badly applied fake tan. To top it off, she's wearing the lowest cut top I have *ever* seen, her thick gold chain vanishing into her cleavage. You simply cannot look away. She announces that she has followed my advice to look more respectable and seems very pleased. When I raise the idea of modesty, she tells me that all men like boobs – magistrates included – and as such she is bound to 'get away with it'. When we go into the courtroom the female chair of the bench peers down at Chantelle contemptuously. Chantelle begins to look self-conscious. Throughout the hearing I can see the magistrates distracted by the cleavage and jewellery.

I am pleased though, because the bench agrees with the Community Service recommendation, concluding that if Chantelle is positively occupied, she might not have time to regale a school full of children.

***

A week later Chantelle is in my office crying.

'The Community Service Order is doing old people's gardens. I can't do it; I'm not fit enough.'

I consider what she has said for a moment and then something clicks. She really does look old for her age and her teeth are a state. I had always assumed this was down to poor hygiene and begin to feel somewhat ashamed of myself.

'I'm always tired, I have to go to bed every afternoon. I do my best to keep on top of everything, but I just don't often feel awake enough. My joints hurt; I'm always in pain. I need to wear lots of make-up because of the rash on my face. My head hurts most of the time, so I can't think. My mouth is so dry I can't speak, and my eyes hurt.'

'Blimey, that's a long list. You've never said anything before, Chantelle. You always look well.'

So many of my clients have woeful lifestyle habits and bad nutrition, I had failed to consider that she might actually be unwell.

'You've never asked. Plus, I have a good sleep before I come here, then go to bed again when I get home.'

I ask if this has been going on for a long time and Chantelle replies, 'Years.'

'Have you been to the doctor?'

'I've been *so* many times, but they just ignore me and basically tell me to stop putting it on. They think I want money, but I just want to feel well.'

Chantelle's usually smiling face is now utterly forlorn. I ask her if she would mind me accompanying her to the GP next time she goes and she agrees. It's completely out of my remit, but I like Chantelle and she is nothing but honest (too honest!). I admit that I hadn't considered her health seriously, and, at any rate, a ten-minute visit to the GP is quicker than a session in my office.

As soon as we enter the surgery, the doctor looks up and gives Chantelle the 'Oh God, not you again' look. Chantelle tries to tell her what's wrong but the doctor completely ignores her, periodically looking at her watch.

I look to Chantelle for permission and she nods. Time to butt in. My nice middle-class voice (thank you, Mum) and professional air has the desired effect, and the doctor sits up and listens. I list Chantelle's symptoms and explain that Chantelle is too tired to cope – I've seen her house and how she lives, which attests to this. I tell her everything that Chantelle has told me and finish off by saying that Chantelle should at least get some blood tests. The doctor agrees.

Chantelle reveals that she has never been offered any tests despite the number of visits to the GP, just ushered out of the surgery before she can really talk. I feel pleased, but also guilty that in one visit I've secured a range of blood tests and a chest X-ray. This should have happened *years* ago.

Ten days later, Chantelle is diagnosed with Lupus, a very serious and debilitating autoimmune condition. The rash on her face, the aching limbs, the severe fatigue, the brain fog — they are all classic signs of the disease.

That evening in my kitchen, surrounded by the washing up I told the kids to do, staring at the broken cooker I asked Tom to mend months ago, wondering if the homework that I've been gently cajoling (blackmailing) the kids into doing has been completed, I fill Tom in on my day. When I stop talking and look to him for an answer, I can tell he hasn't been listening.

I am overcome with intense irritation. I think of Chantelle and how nobody listens to her. Nobody with authority, nobody she has ever turned to for help, has ever *actually* listened to her. She is only ever seen as a nuisance, a caricature, someone not worth listening to. Sure, I think I listen to her, but I probably don't. I judge her. I've made assumptions about her being lazy and incompetent. Not once did I think she was *ill*. Even though the proof of her being unwell was literally plastered across her face.

I reflect upon the informal medical research I do before going to the GP, when I happily give them a list of what might be wrong. I think about the access to information I have, the ability to read and understand it, to be able to articulate how I feel and be understood. I think about how unhealthy most of my clients look, how they eat junk food because nobody has taught them to cook, how they try to explain how they feel, but can't find the right words and how often they act out due to the frustration of not being understood. I think about how I always get my 'rights' because (a) I know what they are, (b) I know how to ask, (c) I present well and (d) I have enough money to have some options.

I'm reminded, yet again, that while there are some genuinely bad people around, more often than not we're dealing with people who are unloved, unwell and rejected by the majority of civil society. Chantelle loves to shout. She clings to the tiny bit of power it gives her, a brief moment in which people might really look at and listen to her. She wants Jade to do well, to be different from her, and things have now started to change. Jade is getting the support she needs in school. Given that Chantelle now has a diagnosed illness, there are charities helping with the children and giving them some respite. With the children's difficulties eased, Chantelle doesn't need to go out and fight in the same way. Plus, the newly qualified social worker has gained some brownie points by having a word with Millie Jackson's mum. The bullying, for now, has stopped.

While it is likely that Chantelle's life will always be chaotic – that is just the way she is – I hope that the extra help and the fact that she has at last been listened to might make her feel just a bit more valued.

Meanwhile, I'm considering buying a megaphone and using that to tell Tom to mend the cooker and get the kids to wash up. Clearly it works!

**

It's a Monday morning a few weeks later and as usual my inbox is full. One of the emails is from Chantelle's social worker. Chantelle and Clive have been arguing in front of the children and this has been affecting their behaviour at school. Sadly, they have now been taken into care to provide

Chantelle and Clive some time to get their life in order. On this occasion, I'm inclined to agree with the social worker's decision. Chantelle and Clive need a set period of space to sort out their issues. Chantelle is devastated. They never really maintained the house after we cleaned it and, on top of their rows, the state of the house meant it was no longer a safe environment for the children, as demonstrated when Chantelle cut her face on a stray pair of scissors one night while sleeping on the sofa. Terrible though it may be, a set period apart from her children might be the push she needs to sort out her house and her life.

I pop in and visit her after work. Last time we spoke she said she was going to split from Clive and his dirty hands, and when I go and visit her today, the deed is done. She knew they were bad for each other. The children need to come first. She has three months to get her act together before Children's Services will consider bringing them home. The plan entails her attending a parenting course and moving house. The current house is terribly overcrowded, which is partly why Chantelle is sleeping on the sofa with scissors. Despite having been offered housing by the local authority, she had previously refused to move because she likes her neighbours. This time she's going to have to take the house or lose her children. When we're chatting, I notice that she looks much healthier now the medication has kicked in and that not only has she ditched Clive, she's also ditched the 'sovs' that turned her fingers black.

Chantelle's house isn't particularly unusual and home visits often feature a certain degree of bedlam. Even more mess than my Tom can make. Even though the atmosphere is loving, there still seems to be an unnerving amount of shouting and commotion. A few years back I worked at the Youth Justice Team where I supervised the Parenting Orders. These were introduced into legislation in 1998 and can be imposed upon the parents of children who have been excluded from school or have criminal convictions. While there were some fathers on the courses, the courts disproportionately impose the orders on mothers, who are more likely to be the main carer, able to solve the problems and, therefore, seen as the most appropriate person to be the subject of an Order.

I used to work with one family who would call each other 'wanker' the way posh families use 'darling', as a term of endearment. The children were all excluded from school, the oldest was shoplifting, and the youngest's favourite game was to play dare on the busy road outside their house. The mum would shrug her shoulders and say, 'kids will be kids'. She didn't seem to have any sense of danger and set no boundaries. The family communicated by loudly talking over each other, never listening to what the other was saying. We started their sessions by choosing new nicknames that weren't aggressive or rude, but they could only think of swear words. We tried to get them to turn down the volume of their voices when they spoke, but they couldn't modulate and struggled to wait their turn to speak. I ended up bringing over a talking stick, and they were only allowed to speak while they were holding it, but they were so desperate to interrupt, they used to fling the stick at each other in frustration and revert to calling each other 'wanker'. Eventually they did manage to take turns to speak and listen, but other weeks they used the stick to hit each other, so I'd have to break up the fight. I loved visiting this family, but it would have been a nightmare to live with them.

Like most of the parents I see, they were initially resistant and offended by having this Order imposed upon them. Who wants to be told how to be a parent? Eventually they would come to appreciate the additional support. Much of the course was held in larger groups and it was lovely to see parents share their experiences and support one another. At the time, I felt like a fraud – I wasn't yet a mum myself and though I had to do a lot of training before delivering the courses I learned every bit as much as they did on the go. Now that I have my own chaotic house, I fully appreciate the hard work they put in to change.

We really did have some successes over the years, with some families never returning to court again and participants remarking how the courses and time out to consider and learn about parenting had completely changed their lives. Obviously, however, for others it didn't work at all, and we continued seeing their children right into adulthood and into their own parenthoods, and sadly continuing into Probation too as they became adult offenders.

I tell Chantelle about the Parenting Orders I used to work on and how she'll end up liking the classes and how prepared she'll be for when the children come back to her. She looks a bit dubious, but mostly optimistic and prepared to try anything. Chantelle is a brave woman. She is bringing up her children in the same way she was brought up. She must unlearn everything she has ever known to get her children back. She must adopt methods and even morals that are alien to her. I can understand that it is arrogant of outside agencies to impose boundaries that are social norms for them but might not be for others, and how confusing it must be to be told the only way you know how to parent isn't right. Ultimately, society wants Chantelle's children to be safe and cared for, to benefit from school so that one day, should they need medical help, a doctor might take them seriously.

I fully appreciate how hard it is to change. We all secretly think that our way is the right way and being told by someone that it isn't immediately puts our backs up. I've been trying for years to make Tom tidier. I try to use the reflective listening methods we use at work to provide further insight. Change has been minimal and today, I am seething with anger. In a hurry to walk the dog and go to work, I look down at the loo and am incensed. I phone Tom, who is already at work. Without any preamble I describe to him in a calm and jovial voice what I have just seen. Beneath the lid, floating in the water, was a brown edifice, surrounded by splatters up the sides with a white tissue arrangement plonked on the top. Muttering 'for fuck's sake' to myself as I pull the chain and clean up the mess (yet again), I resolve that I won't take Max the dog out for a walk this morning but instead wait until his energy levels are high enough to leave him in the garden, where he will inevitably start digging up Tom's precious bowling green lawn. I describe this to Tom in detail, painting a vivid picture of the vast, cavernous holes that will be awaiting him on his return home before angrily plonking the phone down again and leaving the house.

That evening Tom informs me that he had been at another company working in their open plan office and that his phone was on speaker. He had tried to take the phone off speaker, but in his haste, dropped it on the floor instead, where my loud voice describing the turd continued to entertain everyone else nearby. Later, someone at the kettle had referred to him as 'Skiddy' and chuckled to themselves before walking off. Tom was not pleased. I was though. I hoped that he might finally stop being a naughty boy and clean up after himself in future.

Tom comes from a very relaxed family. The first time he took me home to meet his parents, his elderly mother, Mary, was in the kitchen washing her bosoms in the sink. They were covered in soap suds, as was the hand that she reached out to me to shake and say hello, her boobs still dripping in water. My sister-in-law, Florence, recalls a similar first meeting with Tom, who she bumped into on the stairs at Tom's parents' house. Tom was naked and on his way to the loo (probably to leave a mess) and, without a trace of embarrassment, he held out his hand to shake hers and introduce himself. Tom's younger brother Mike, while similar-looking to Tom, is much more conventional. He is also tidy. Mary always said she practised on Tom and got it right by Mike. When we visit Florence and Mike in their immaculate house, I see Mike eying Tom and the empty cups and litter that have accumulated around his ankles with the magnetic pull of planets around the sun, before he gives up and scurries around Tom and clears it away. Tom is totally oblivious to the hum of activity around him, and I can tell that people have been clearing up after him his entire life. I know that I could use every single method available to encourage him to be tidy and that not one will be successful. I am constantly reminded of how difficult it is to change behaviour that is so fully entrenched and what a lot of hard work is involved for the people we see. I know that Chantelle can do it though. She will get the ultimate prize: her children.

7

George

'Fuck, cunt, arousal, sex, cock, clit, wank, cum, tits, bollocks, masturbate, penis!'

Mick is stomping around the office doing his ritual. The usually mild-mannered man hasn't gone mad, though the words jar coming from his mouth. It's an unconventional exercise he learned at university in the 1980s when training to be a Probation Officer, designed to prepare students for working with sex offenders. It might sound bizarre, but the idea is to help desensitise you enough that you can perhaps see the human being beyond the heinous act. Each morning started with the students going around the classroom swearing and hurling sexual insults at each other, the terms becoming more outrageous as the year went on, until eventually the giggling stopped. There was no more embarrassment, no more flinching. I wish the practice had continued, but by the time I was training in the nineties, there was no such preparation.

Today, we are consciously trying to use more appropriate and accurate language when discussing sexual violence. However, as Probation Officers we are often, by definition, discussing inappropriate things, things that make us wince.

Unlike Mick, most of us have not been prepared for the horrors we hear when working with sex offenders. We just get on with it, feeling (and probably looking) shocked until we no longer are. Sex offenders are usually highly skilled manipulators – they have spent years perfecting the craft of persuading people to do things they don't want to do. They search for chinks of fear in people's faces, scanning for signs of weakness. They are skilled at controlling a situation. This is why I started using Mick's method to keep my face blank. It helps me numb myself to what I'm about to hear.

I usually read the offender's file at home before meeting for the first time and it's here that I allow myself to cry. I can hear my own children laughing in front of the television in the room next door and I feel afraid. What if they bumped into someone like this? I study the sanitised version of events, punctuated with cold, forensic phrases like 'digital insertion' and I instinctively know that the person who transcribed the interview and took statements adopted the same protective detachment I need. But they will soon move on to the next offender. Only Probation Officers keep seeing sex offenders, week after week, month after month – listening to their crimes, persuading them to stop. My emotions, my disgust, don't have a useful role in these situations. The goal is to protect members of the public, though most of them don't know we exist.

Probation Officers actively encourage all sex offenders, including paedophiles, to verbalise their fantasies. This must be carefully managed. It's important these men – and yes, they mostly are men – don't become aroused. They need to know that they are talking to someone who cannot possibly be manipulated, groomed or coerced, and yet they should feel free to talk without judgement. The ability to maintain a totally blank and impassive face when underneath you are thinking 'fucking hell, this is vile, I'm going to be sick', is vital for this to succeed.

Much of our work with sex offenders is underpinned by motivational interviewing. We build up trust, and allow them to talk without interruption while ensuring there are boundaries and no impression of agreement with the behaviour they describe. We cannot appear disgusted because if they feel bad about themselves, they won't engage and, most importantly, they won't *change*. Person-centred therapy – listening, patience and understanding – help the offender to fully accept what is 'really' going on so they can start to understand their motivations and choose to address these, while the Probation Officer balances the requisite care and control.

I start every conversation with 'You can tell me *anything*. I've heard it all before. I can't be shocked. It'll be good to get it off your chest after all these years. We can start to work through what is legal and acceptable and what isn't. It'll help you to stop getting into trouble.' Sadly, after many years of working with sex offenders, it's true, I am unshockable.

I have found that most offenders justify and excuse their behaviour, minimising and shifting blame. The internet offender 'got sent those images', rarely admitting they sought them out and paid for them. Rapists blame and shame the victims with excuses about what they were wearing. I've heard paedophiles describe children as behaving 'provocatively'. Violent exes argue it was okay to force their former partners into sex because 'they've done it before'. However, despite some commonalities depending on the nature of the crime, in my experience, sex offenders fall into three categories.

First, there are those who say they have a sexual preference for children, much like a heterosexual prefers members of the opposite sex, though this is a contentious area. There are studies that suggest there are some anomalies in the brains of this group, providing a deep-rooted, biological reason for the commission of offences.* But paedophiles are not routinely checked for this and so we have scant idea as to how significant a part their neurobiology plays.

The second group have an absolute sense of entitlement and get a kick from the power abuse affords them. They firmly believe it is their right to commit whatever offences they like, and because of this, they are unlikely to ever change. It is vital for the Probation Officer not to look scared by these offenders, because they can also 'get off' on taking control of the interview, especially if they think they can get under our skin. Most of all, they want you to think they are actually in the third group: those who could change.

The third group know they are different to most people and have a feeling that things aren't quite right: they'd like to change, but don't know how. Being a sex offender is lonely and the stigma reinforces their self-loathing. They want to be loved but feel unworthy. They confuse sexual gratification

---

* Lara Speer et al., 'Sexual preference for prepubescent children is associated with enhanced processing of child faces in juveniles', *European Child & Adolescent Psychiatry*, 31(2), February 2022, pp. 261–274.

with love, but don't know how to change. They are open to help, and they want to be supported.*

In my experience, the third group is more common, however, the second group will use all their powers of manipulation to try to persuade you they are also in the third group. Since it's important not to be manipulated, I approach every offender with the same level of scepticism, only allowing myself to feel optimistic when their behaviour *actually* changes.

***

George fits into the third category. He wants to stop; he is sick of being in and out of prison and just wants to be 'normal'. While he wrestles with the immensity of his crimes, he wants to explore why he committed them. I really think he has the potential to change. It is important for all the groups to be able to talk about their offences, so that we can assess which group they belong in. It's an absolute tightrope of presenting an unshakable exterior, when underneath all you feel is revulsion. The Probation Officer might be the first person the offender has ever been candid with; it's not exactly something they can talk about with friends and family. During our sessions, George, and those like him, can be open about what they have done and listened to. If we immediately condemn

---

*   Strictly speaking there is also a fourth group, female sex offenders. But these only account for around two per cent of sexual offence convictions. See *Women and the Criminal Justice System 2023*, Ministry of Justice, 30 January 2025: https://assets.publishing.service.gov.uk/media/679b44b5f2c688b4b630eab4/Statistics_on_Women_and_the_Criminal_Justice_System_2023.pdf.

them, they'll never fully process why things are or are not okay. So, though I may be filled with horror, I still listen, trying to look almost bored. I only start to challenge an offender once trust has been built.

In a strange way, it's a privilege to be trusted with their absolute deepest thoughts and admissions, to be part of the journey that will stop them committing more offences in the future. George is part way through a long parole term, and we've been meeting regularly for two years. He is starting to explore what motivated him to offend and trying to change. As such, he has no qualms about describing what he has done in excruciating detail and every meeting is a battle to resist sticking my fingers in my ears.

George is an elderly, overweight man. A life of chain-smoking has stained his teeth, lips and fingers a faded yellow. He is a convicted paedophile with a long criminal history. His current conviction is for the rape and sexual assault of two boys aged fourteen and thirteen. I feel the same horror that everyone feels about his offences but have to put that away if I'm to work with him effectively. If he had been anywhere near my son, I would want to kill him with my bare hands. The thought still pops up from time to time, so I concentrate on the fact that I might be able to help him change his behaviour and prevent him from harming someone else's son in the future. He talks about his offences in detail every week, trying to work out what made him do it and how he can stop himself.

I spend a lot of my time with him, controlling my face and trying not to absorb too many details of what he's saying because these make me nauseous. I ask him about why he gave himself permission to commit the offences in the first place. In George's mind, he had proper relationships with these boys and describes loving, consensual sex. I think he genuinely believes it, and just can't grasp that his sexual activities were with children, not adults, and they could never be consensual, the imbalance of power so totally weighted in his favour. Despite not yet understanding this, he has a genuine motivation to change. Therefore, in a strange way, he is a joy to work with and, against my better judgement, I like him. Mick can't get his head around why I see him as a worthy cause and describes him as a 'stinky fat old man'.

As a boy, George was sexually abused by his father. It was kept secret from the wider family, who had no idea what was happening to him. George believes that nobody even *suspected* his father was abusing him, and he never felt able to confide in his mother. George's father persuaded him that it was because he was the favourite son. George felt uncomfortable – it didn't feel 'right' – but he enjoyed the attention, and the secrecy made him feel special. He admits that, despite the dark feeling lurking in the pit of his stomach, he was physically aroused and so felt complicit. At school he befriended a younger boy and engaged in sexual activity at the back of the playing field with him. In hindsight, George recognises he coerced this boy, but at the time he believed the other boy was enjoying the attention. George still struggles to comprehend the full meaning of consent: he claims that his father did not abuse him, that he said 'yes', failing to understand that, as a child, he could not give consent.

After George's father stopped abusing him in his late teens, George continued to abuse younger boys. He tells me the victims were willing participants, but a shadow of doubt casts over his face. I ask him to concentrate on the feelings he had when his own father was abusing him; to consider that ingrained feeling that what was happening wasn't right. Did he *really* give his father permission?

George brushes the comments off and expands upon his recent victims. The boys were frequent visitors to his flat – he hadn't cajoled them, he informs me, they visited of their own free will. I ask about the money and sweets that he gave them, and he seems offended that the boys might have been motivated by something other than the pleasure of his company. George enjoyed talking to the boys; he had always found it easier to communicate with children and never really knew how to talk to adults.

This makes me sad. George is an intelligent man – he is well-read and interested in the arts, spirituality and faith. He isn't a one-dimensional monster; we discuss many things that have nothing to do with sex. If you met him in another context, you would never suspect his perversions. I find it difficult not to like him. Part of his supervision is to encourage other elements of his personality to flourish. He doesn't appear able to acknowledge that he is likeable. His self-loathing is so fully entrenched. He tells me that adults don't like him. I suggest that adults don't like him because of his crimes rather than his personality. But he is also disliked by the staff at the probation hostel where he resides. This is because, unlike those of the other residents, his room is filled with books, pictures and bric-a-brac. By contrast, everyone else's room looks like a prison cell, with no personal effects. He maintains it is his home and stubbornly refuses to clear it out. The staff see this as another example of him being unwilling to change, as opposed to evidence of an interior life.

Meanwhile, he continues to suggest that the children he abused liked him and what he did. He goes so far as to say that his victims will have been devastated by his incarceration because they loved him. Despite his seemingly genuine desire to change, he just can't seem to get it in his head that it was wrong, that young boys don't want to have sex with him. Sometimes I want to shout at him, but this won't make him change. Confronting people in this way, all guns blazing, just makes them dig their heels in, so I must continue with the soft approach week in, week out. Nudging him to think about what it is to be a child, the importance of being safe, gently encouraging behaviour that will make him happy by preventing a return to prison, but also keep children safe. For him to stop offending altogether, he must truly understand the nature of positive, appropriate relationships between adults and children.

The only people he can fully and deeply reveal his feelings to are me and other sex offenders. He is currently under investigation because he has been spending a lot of time with the other sex offenders in the hostel and there is concern that they are starting a paedophile ring. George reassures me that they are simply a bunch of old men who haven't got any other friends and none of them can be bothered to have sex anymore anyway. George is lonely and, understandably, he wants some friends, but nobody in the hostel will be mates with him because he's a 'nonce', so the only people he can befriend are other 'nonces'. His reasons are plausible. But it adds another layer of suspicion. It is impossible to know for sure if he's telling the truth. He maintains that children seduced him, and our debate continues every week.

I've put him on another sex offender programme in the community as well as seeing me. This week, George tells me that he has been doing his best not to look at children at all but is finding it difficult as they are 'everywhere', but lately if he passes one on the street, he closes his eyes. He looks pleased with himself. I've decided to use a different tack and have brought along a mirror. I put it in front of him and ask him to describe what he sees. He is honest: a fat, balding seventy-year-old stares back at him, a splatter of sauce staining the front of his jumper. I ask him if he truly believes that a fourteen-year-old would fancy him. He doesn't answer. I want to throttle him.

Reading this back now, I can't understand why I like George. It's a bit like being teacher to a willing and enthusiastic pupil who really wants to learn how to do fractions but just can't work it out. It's a challenge, but I pray that one day he will understand, and the satisfaction of that breakthrough will be immense.

Despite the hurdles, there are small glimmers of hope. I've decided that for the next few weeks we are going to concentrate on his father's abuse, a subject he has managed to avoid until now. He agrees but looks distinctly uncomfortable. He says that his mouth is dry and asks for water. He looks down at the floor and fidgets. I try to encourage him and he looks away. He tries to defend his father by saying that he was a 'lovely man really'. I ask George if he really believes this. He doesn't reply. We sit in silence again, waiting for George to find the words, but they don't come. And as before, he manages to wrangle his way out, changing the subject yet again. He describes how one of his victims had suggested they could give George a massage. Massages appear to be a universal ploy with sex offenders, no matter their social position. Just look at Harvey Weinstein and Jeffrey Epstein. I point out that it was likely the other way round, that he requested the massage. George concedes but hastily adds that the boy was 'up for it'. I roll my eyes in exasperation and try not to think about all the times that I've enjoyed evenings with our children and their friends where we've done each other's hair and I've given them back massages. The innocent fun and the joy of touching my children is routinely spoiled by stories I hear at work.

After a couple of years of repetitive work and mounting frustration, George finally breaks down. He describes how he loved his father and desperately wanted to please him, recalls the shiver of dread whenever his father walked into his bedroom at night and how he has always felt that this was the only way to be loved by him, by anyone. He talks about the mixture of relief and the disappointment he felt when the abuse ended. George has spent his life trying to retrieve that sense of being loved but had never really succeeded. He is sobbing now, for what he has done to other boys, how he has transferred his pain to them. We have finally got somewhere – this is the 'lightbulb' moment. George has admitted to the harm he has done and knows *why* he must change.

***

Regardless of the importance and relief of this breakthrough, I'm exhausted after spending so much time cajoling George to this point. Probation Officers must learn to compartmentalise, otherwise we would drive ourselves mad. We must completely switch off from work once we step outside the office. However, this process is seldom smooth, and I've had colleagues who have needed to go into counselling because they are so scared of enjoying giving their children a bath after years of working with sex offenders. Obviously, the Probation Service doesn't pay for it. Some people are robbed of the simplest domestic pleasures. In view of this, we all do our best to make light of the darkest, sickest aspects and laughter regularly echoes down the corridor after the worst days. We discuss what we'd really like to do to our clients, like keep them in prison and never see them again. We sometimes talk about the banality of our own sex lives just to check that we are 'normal' and then we all laugh together about how boring we are. In reality, the laughter is a sticking plaster for the pain we feel, alongside the anti-depressants we're all on. More and more often, as funds are slashed and caseloads pile up, the laughter gives way to tears.

It is doubly important to look after your own wellbeing if you work with dangerous and cruel offenders. And rather than become an alcoholic like many Probation Officers, I settle on the rather more genteel hobbies of beekeeping and tending to my allotment. It's such a lovely place to unwind – whether you're standing by your fork nattering to old men about carrots or donning your suit and looking at the beehive, the air clouding with bees as soon as the lid is off, while the humans gradually evacuate. Everyone seems 'normal' here, where being boring about carrots is the gravest of crimes imaginable. It's at the allotment that I appreciate how abnormal most of the conversations I have at work truly are. There are couples gently talking and it doesn't look like they are about to hit each other. Some of the old granddads are helping the children to plant things and one has even bought their grandchild a bee suit so they can investigate his hive and when they do, he puts a protective arm around her shoulder where it remains in an appropriate spot.

Banal, pleasant stuff. You realise that most people in the world are really quite nice. As time passes, it's harder to go to the allotment – I'm busy with the pervy granddads rather than the sweet ones – so in a magnanimous gesture of love, I hand the allotment over to my parents. I'm not if sure if they want it, but I'd still like the organic veg and to pop down to the pub for the veg swap every month. I wish I could give them my job instead. I am still keeping bees though, because there's an excitement to keeping bees, an edge of danger. (That being said, I never get stung, although they seem to like stinging Tom.)

I am lucky. I have had so much love in my life. Honestly, I never really appreciated how wonderful that is until I started working with people who don't. Like most people who are happy, I've just taken it for granted. My parents are stable and the lack of arguing and chaos wasn't as boring as I'd believed as a child, it was just reassuring and safe. Looking back, those trips to castles were for me and I'm grateful. My husband is fantastic, I can go on and on about him being a slob (oh my God he really is) in the sure knowledge that he won't beat me to a pulp if I moan at him. And the children, well, I adore them. I sometimes think we must look like a fish finger advert when we have our dinner, sat neatly about the table laughing and chatting. We rarely shout at each other; disputes are generally settled through conversation and debate. There is no price for this feeling, of being safe in your own home. Unfortunately, a great many people in our society don't feel this. Those of us who do should thank our lucky stars.

Before having children, I envisaged a big family kitchen with a blackboard on the wall for reminders and a fridge covered in fridge magnets holding up a collage of personal notes, drawings and photos. For some strange reason these two things encapsulated motherhood for me. The first photo on our fridge was a scan of our unborn child, artfully stuffed under a magnet from the National Trust, a gift from my parents. After my daughter was born, we collected more magnets from around the country. Pictures of hand- and footprints went up, then splodges of paint and squiggles of pen, until the kids went to school; then there was an array of writing and pictures. The blackboard was papered with love hearts, doodled on the corners of lists and notes, illustrating just how much we loved each other. As my children got older, the love notes and hearts died down, replaced by the reminders about the dentist and what to buy at Sainsbury's. Lately, however, my daughter has started using it again. Last week there was a big love heart coloured in carefully in bright pink with 'I love Cameron', a good-looking young lad in her class at school. A few days later it was scribbled out and replaced by 'Cameron is dead to me', once she'd gone off him again.

George has never enjoyed these simple pleasures. His life has been dominated by sexual abuse, as both victim and perpetrator. He has spent his whole life looking over his shoulder, desperate to be loved and not knowing how. He has spent years in prison. He was never given the chance at a normal life and he, in turn, has ruined other lives. He will never know the peace that I have enjoyed. The peace that only comes from constant and respectful love and stability.

George died in a nursing home aged eighty-two. After our time together, he never committed another offence.

8

Abdul

I can't breathe.

Each breath floods my lungs with the stench of petrol, vomit, excrement and rotting meat. I feel like my body is being consumed by the smell, like it is solid. That it has become part of me. It is stiflingly hot and pitch black, not even a chink of light. The engine vibrates, a steady hum; I can hear voices murmuring in the background. Closer are the sounds of wailing and groaning. It sounds like animals. I am disorientated. I don't know how long I've felt like this.

I long to see something, but nothing works – our torches and phones are long dead. I have never known darkness like this. I don't know if my eyes are open or closed. I want to be sick, but my stomach's empty. Besides, I can't be sick, I can't add to the noise. I must remain silent.

Am I dead? Is this hell? Fluid is running down my legs, I'm soaked in it. It smells like urine, but it is too cold. I remember how it felt when I was a baby. The feeling in my nappy when it was wet. In the darkness I can remember every detail of my life. The faces of my family; the sandy soil surrounding our house, filling the gaps between my toes. My sisters' laughter as they play. My mother's smiling face, so close to mine that I can feel her breath as she bathes me and changes me. My father looking over her shoulder, chuckling at me; the love in his eyes. I sit in my pushchair, studying my grandfather as he tends his goats in the sun, content. I can feel the warmth on my face, filled with happiness.

This is before the gunshots echo – my grandfather is gone, and my parents are crying.

My father rests next to me now, in the darkness. We have been lying together on an old mattress. I remember. It is his urine that has soaked through my trousers, but he is dead. It is the smell of his body that has filled my nostrils. His body has started to rot, the last signs that he was once alive leaking out of him, now cold. I want to move away from him, but there is no room. There are other people on mattresses all around. I want to scream, but there is the cacophony of other people screaming so I stay silent. I imagine my father smiling at me over my mother's shoulder, playing peekaboo. The memory of it makes me smile.

The engine stops. The door opens and we squint. It is night outside, but it feels bright by comparison. We can't move; our bodies too stiff. They pull us out by our arms. As we try to stand, some people fall to the ground. But I am strong. I am determined to stand. My life depends upon me standing. I'm alive, I can't die. The mattresses are dragged out. One of them has my father on it. Other people's fathers lie motionless too, some of them roll off the mattresses onto the tarmac road. Where are we?

We are given shovels and told to dig, but our arms are weak. I remind myself that I am strong. I must bury my father. I love my father, and he was always strong. But why wasn't he strong enough to stay with me? I am angry with him. They are shouting at us to dig faster; 'the hole isn't deep enough'. I can hear the

ABDUL

people digging around me praying. I want to pray too, but I can't remember the words.

We stand at the edge of a straight empty road, fields all around us. There are no buildings. Should I run? I'm too scared. I head back into the darkness. There is no mattress now, the floor is hard. The smell of my dead father has gone. At first, I'm relieved, but then I miss it. I want him back. Where did I bury my father? The engine roars back to life. There is screaming, crying, groaning all around. It is met by shouts to be quiet. I am holding someone; we cling to each other. They feel warm. We cry together.

Many days later, they are yelling at us to get out again. This time there are streetlights all around, blinding us. We blink in the light. They hand out new clothes and force the children to move away from the adults, their arms stretched out to each other. They are crying and looking pleadingly at one another. Pushing back a feeling of relief that all of us are now alone without parents, I see my school friend; we stand close together, our bodies touching from shoulders to feet. We grab each other's hands and hold tight hoping that nobody sees. We are pressed into another dark place. This time a few chinks of light creep through. As the engine starts again, we try to look out – bright pinpricks of streetlights speed past us through the tiny holes. They shout at us to be silent; we are scared to breathe. Then we are on the water. There is chatter all around us, then silence. The engines growl, I feel sick because of the motion of the water, but I can't make a sound.

When we next stop, it is quiet. The doors open. We must hurry. We stumble out. It smells of petrol again, it's familiar. I breathe in, but behind the petrol there is fresh air, no smell of rotting flesh. I take gulps of it. I feel like I've never breathed before.

We stand in a huddle, but there are only six of us. Where did everyone else go? Once there were forty.

Suddenly, flashing blue lights are blaring towards us out of the twilight. Someone is talking, they aren't shouting. They are talking with kind voices, they have blankets, and they feel warm and soft, they wrap us up in them. We get into the cars with the blue lights.

We are alive.

***

Abdul is sitting in my office. He has just finished describing his journey to England. His voice has remained steady. I handed him the tissues I expected him to cry into, but he refused. He says he is strong but I wonder if it is because he has no tears left.

He was fourteen when he made that journey. And eighteen now.

The journey from Afghanistan had taken sixty days. Abdul travelled through countless countries: Pakistan, Iran, Turkey, Croatia, Slovenia, Italy and France, though he had no idea where he was most of the time. All sense of time and place were lost to the darkness, first inside an old petrol tanker. Many had died on the way, their bodies dumped by the side of the road. In France, the children were transferred to a lorry for the final part of the journey to the UK. The traffickers believed that the children were more likely to be granted asylum if they were unaccompanied. So six of them were abandoned at a petrol station in Kent and taken away by police.

ABDUL

Before Abdul left Afghanistan, most of his male relatives had already been murdered. His father was receiving death threats and knew that he and Abdul would be next. If he and his young son were to survive, they needed to get out. He hoped that once settled they could secure asylum, before sending for the women in the family. Abdul remembers saying goodbye to his weeping mother and sisters. He was fearful for their safety, but optimistic that, as women, they might be spared. At fourteen, he had never left his village before, but he was bright and already had a good command of English, taught to him by his father. They sold their land and his grandfather's goats to pay the traffickers.

He has spent the last three years trying to find his grandmother, mother and sisters. He was in contact with them for the first year he was here, but one day their phone number stopped working. The Red Cross were eventually able to visit his address back in Afghanistan but found the house empty – no furniture or belongings and no sign of life. Abdul doesn't know if they are alive or dead. There is no trace of them and it is too dangerous for him to return and search for them. He says that sometimes he wishes he could return to the darkness of the lorry where his memories were clear and he could remember those last hugs with his family, what they felt like, what they smelt like. Even their faces are starting to fade from his memory.

Abdul has been here four years, but his asylum application is yet to be decided. He tells me that everyone has been kind, and getting arrested hasn't been bad because of the people he has met. When we start to talk about his 'offence', I feel ashamed of our country – he isn't a criminal. He's just a scared teenager who came here out of desperation.

After arriving in the UK, Abdul was placed in a house with other refugee children and an Afghan carer. They were allotted a social worker, Dave, who helped with their care and applications to remain in this country. In the meantime, they weren't entitled to any money until they turned eighteen. After this, Abdul started getting £49.18 per week[*] on an Aspen (Asylum Support Enablement) card. Much like a debit card, it can be used to cover the cost of food, clothing and toiletries, and the Home Office can and do monitor what the money is being spent on. Cash – to an agreed limit – can also be taken from a cash point, but this may incur a charge. Asylum seekers are encouraged to take up voluntary work but forbidden from undertaking paid work and therefore that £49.18 is their only income. That's just £2,557.36 a *year*. While Abdul has been here for four years his application *still* hasn't been heard. He is desperate to work as, unsurprisingly, the Aspen card doesn't cover even the most basic essentials. But he never stole.

Abdul desperately needed a job. To circumnavigate the fact that he wasn't allowed to work, he found a job at a fast-food outlet where he was paid in food rather than cash. One evening, when he and his colleagues were cleaning up after closing, some drunk local men started pounding on the windows demanding to be served. They were politely informed that the takeaway was closed. The men continued to bang on the windows in a threatening manner, so restaurant staff called the police. But an hour and a half later, the police still

---

[*] 'Asylum Support', Gov.UK: https://www.gov.uk/asylum-support/what-youll-get. Accessed 28 July 2025.

hadn't arrived, and the men outside were still hammering on the windows.

Scared out of his wits and fearful that he may have breached the terms of his asylum application by working, despite not being paid, Abdul decided he would try to make a run for it and go home. His manager told him to use a broom for protection. He opened the door and ran. Everything that follows was captured on CCTV and, like the police and Crown Prosecution Service, I have seen the incident in full. Once in the street Abdul is encircled by the local men who shout 'Paki! Fuck off back to Pakistan!' Abdul looks terrified, waving the broom around in the air, trying to fend them off. He never touches any of them. He's clearly trying to appear menacing, but instead he looks even more vulnerable. Finally, the police arrive and round them all up into the van – including Abdul.

Watching the CCTV footage, I feel a deep rage. The injustice of the police slinging the victim of racist abuse, who simply wanted to get home, into the same van as his tormentors and then charging him with affray. It barely made sense. The police and Crown Prosecution Service saw the same CCTV footage as me, where Abdul was very clearly targeted, and yet they pursued the charge. The only conclusion I can draw from it is that the 'system' has the same views as the perpetrators of this crime. Now Abdul is here sitting in front of me for a Pre-Sentence Report interview. I feel ashamed of the organisation I am representing.

It helps that Abdul displays no bitterness and takes it all in his stride. He is a lovely, gentle young man. He speaks perfect English, complete with a local accent. He has built his life here, been to school and made friends. He enjoys close bonds with the other Afghans in his house. His social worker can't speak more highly of him.

At the court hearing the magistrates obviously agree and give him a conditional discharge, while his co-defendants, the local men, are given Community Service Orders. His solicitor thinks he should appeal, but Abdul doesn't wish to cause trouble and, despite his innocence and advice from his solicitor, fears any complaint could mean he is deported, so he says no. He just wants to forget about the whole thing. I'd love to continue to see him, but in view of his conditional discharge, my work with him is done.

**

Abdul has supported Manchester United his entire life and continues to squeeze himself into the beloved number ten football shirt he travelled to the UK in. His favourite thing is to play football in the local park with the other lads in his house share. I promise to go and watch next time I'm walking the dog there. A few weeks later, as promised, I go and stand on the sidelines and watch them playing. His social worker, Dave, is there too. I tell Dave what an amazing job he has and how rewarding it must be to work with unaccompanied children like Abdul. He responds: 'I haven't had a decent night's sleep since I took the job. I want to bring every one of them home, but my wife won't let me.' I know exactly how he feels.

We're busy chatting when some women come and stand next to us and start bitching. 'Bloody foreigners. We can't even enjoy our own parks anymore without them showing up.'

I'm incensed; Dave gives me a nudge. He knows I'm about to argue with them. He tells me how many times he's tried to tell people, but they don't listen. They won't change their minds. 'They'll continue to complain about these lovely brave young lads who have gone through so much. It's not worth the aggro,' he says, 'and that's another reason I can't sleep at night.'

Dave explains the difficulties of keeping the 'safe' houses safe and the complaints they get from residents about housing migrants. He tells me that they have encouraged relationships with the closest neighbours, sharing Afghan food and stories. Abdul and his friends have been helping in their gardens. He describes their growing, positive bonds in the community and how the neighbours adore the young lads. Yet they continually face resistance from others. For the adults in hotels, who have had equally harrowing journeys, it is worse, with local campaigns to get them evicted.

Dave concentrates on the positives – the fundraising, the organisations staffed by volunteers who are helping asylum seekers to integrate and make a life here – but he is saddened and scared by the those who continue to seek to make things difficult with threats and complaints.

It takes another year for Abdul to be granted asylum. He is now nineteen and can follow his dream of going to university to study international politics. He thinks he might get answers through his course and eventually help other people like him. Saying goodbye to Dave and his Afghan carer, he cautiously shares his new address with the Red Cross, 'just in case' his mother contacts him. He has not heard any news of her or his sisters for five years, but he will never lose hope.

Dave is still working with refugees and the locals are still complaining about them.

Abdul is a man now and I haven't seen him in the park lately, but I often think of him. Despite the horrifying traumas he has endured, he really was as strong as he said he was, and I feel sure that he will have made a good life for himself. He wanted to do it in honour of his parents, who sacrificed everything to save his life.

***

We're off on a weekend break, dragging our knackered old camper van out of the driveway, mattress haphazardly chucked into the back. I've been running around the supermarket buying provisions and, after double-checking we've got the dog and his bag of treats, we begin our journey to Kent. The engine releases a foul petroleum stench back into the van, so the windows are all open. The dog and I have our heads out and his ears are gently flapping in the breeze. Tom has purchased some new outdoor clothing. He dons every type of waterproof, from his hat to his boots. He thinks his new gear will help him walk further. I have a hunch the added weight will achieve the exact opposite but remain diplomatically silent. As we speed along the A2 near Canterbury we pass some petrol stations, and I wonder if one of them is where Abdul was dropped off when he arrived in the country.

After we find somewhere to park up, we have a walk. It's been raining. Tom proudly gives me a twirl, excited to wear his new collection of waterproof gear. It is a beautiful, serene evening and the wet fields shimmer in the twilight after the rain has stopped. We hold hands, feeling content. Back in the van settling down for the night, I notice that it still smells of petrol and Tom is wearing his gaiters.

9

Maisy

'Can you turn that snooze button off?'

Lying in bed with Tom, neither of us can be bothered to move and he's pressed the snooze button at least four times. We're pressed together and I feel so much love for this familiar, beautiful face. He opens his eyes from slumber, tries to tempt me into more than a cuddle and exhales his morning hay breath into my face, dispelling all sexy thoughts. I push him off and get up. I've got a home visit at Barry's to get to.

Barry is one of Mick's clients and, despite my begging for Barry to be given a week off while Mick is on holiday, I have to pay him a visit in his stead. Barry is a prolific flasher and public masturbator who likes nothing more than to press himself against unsuspecting commuters in the morning crush. Saving the travellers from this odious occurrence one day a week is Mick, who gets up early and sees Barry in the office at 7.30 a.m. By the time their appointment is over, most commuters are safely on the train headed to work, leaving Barry disgruntled at missing his daily fix.

He is a familiar face in the town – flashers aren't hard to miss – and to be avoided like the plague. He's well into his sixties and has a good twenty years' 'experience'. Nobody knows when or why he started doing it and we have scant information about him, despite his being an almost permanent fixture on probation. Barry has never fallen prey to the temptation to talk about himself. He refuses to tell us any of his history and, apart from the thick file which contains notes about his many arrests and periods in prison or on probation, we know nothing about his upbringing, background or what motivates him. Living alone in a council flat with no known family or friends, he is an enigma.

He only chats about his ailments, for which he refuses to see the doctor until he needs a sick note to get his benefits. He doesn't work because of his poor health (and nobody in their right mind would ever give him a job).

Currently on probation for his most recent sequence of exposures, he must be seen weekly. This level of supervision is crucial as exposure can sometimes escalate to more serious crimes, but it hasn't always been taken seriously by the police. For example, it was revealed that Sarah Everard's killer had exposed himself to female staff at a McDonald's twice just days before murdering her. Had these offences been investigated properly, she might still be alive. I once discovered, unofficially from a friendly police officer, that one rapist I worked with – who ostensibly had a squeaky-clean criminal record – had previously been arrested (but not charged) for exposure. It seems 'he's just a flasher' is an easy excuse to do nothing. Taking seemingly 'minor' sexual offences seriously might not only prevent escalation, but allow women to feel safe in public spaces.

The school run takes priority for me, so I can't see him until after the morning commute at the station. Given that many other offenders recognise him, he can't come into the office during opening hours given the risk of getting beaten up and called a 'nonce' by others in the waiting room. That's why Mick sees him early. Consequently, I've been instructed to carry out a home visit as the Probation Service feels more comfortable forfeiting the safety of their staff rather than risking Barry getting a beating on their turf.

Barry wears shorts all year round, revealing ulcers he refuses to have treated. Sitting in his filthy living room, I politely decline the offer of tea from a dirty cup and wonder what to discuss this week, all while trying not to stare at his missing teeth. As I run through my questions, I let my mind wander – have I got time to go to Sainsbury's on the way back to the office? If I'm quick I could squeeze that in before Maisy comes for her appointment, and I can get her some breakfast while I'm there. Pondering what to cook for dinner, I suddenly notice Barry's hand moving up and down in his shorts. I stop asking him inane questions and hastily leave. Looking up at his flat as I get in the car, I see he is pressing his flaccid penis on the window, shouting 'I can pay for it, you know.' Delightful.

He's done me a favour bringing the visit to a premature end; I've time to pop into Sainsbury's after all.

Maisy is already napping in the waiting room when I arrive. She rouses and comes into my office, where she immediately continues to, as heroin users say, 'gouch out'. Following her morning hit, she is almost catatonic, sitting in the chair with her eyes rolling around, unable to communicate at all. Like every week, I catch up on some paperwork while she stares into nothingness. She doesn't look comfortable slumped across the desk, mouth agape, but she's safe. Her once pretty face is now ravaged by heroin use and, as she drifts in and out of consciousness with her eyes wide open, she presents as a ghoulish figure. This weekly routine used to fill me with the fear that she was going to die before my eyes, but I've become strangely accustomed to it and know that within an hour she'll be awake and waiting to hungrily devour the sandwiches I bought her. I'm pleased that I was able to buy her something decent.

Maisy is a child of a family well known to the courts. Both of her parents have a long history of offending, as does her brother, who is their obvious favourite. Maisy, however, is different to the others. Constantly jeered at and called a 'swot' by her family, she enjoyed school and was an academically able girl. Encouraged by the teachers, who could see her potential, and against the odds, she gained a place at university to study Geography. Pleased to get away, she hoped for a completely different life in another town – to make something of herself. Meanwhile, there was great consternation within her family about moving on to further education. They were embarrassed and uncomfortable about her intelligence and 'weird, lefty ideas', and told her she never fitted in anyway. So far, so *Matilda*.

Maisy loved the academic side of university but found it difficult to fit in, feeling as different to her peers there as she had done at home with her family. Lacking the support she'd enjoyed from her teachers at school, she began to struggle. Compounding this was her precarious financial situation; in a new city, away from family, she didn't know where to turn for help.

Aware that her mother had dabbled in prostitution when the family were short of money, she wondered if this could be an option to address her own financial shortcomings. Not sure where to start, she went to the local red-light district and asked one of the sex workers there for help. Despite her rough background, she was an innocent young woman of eighteen and, when advised that if she was going to have sex with strangers, she wouldn't be able to do it sober, she agreed to buy drugs to help her through it. A few days later, Maisy was given heroin to help her cope with her first 'job'. Having taken the edge off her fear, her first evening didn't seem too bad and she made enough money to pay the rent for a week. Her career as a sex worker had begun. As her heroin use also increased, she was unable to engage with university and became further indebted until she was forced to return home to the family fold.

Finally, Maisy had become 'one of them' and her family welcomed her back with open arms. Her parents weren't at all perturbed by her situation, seeing it as a normal way to live. Maisy enjoyed the positive attention she was getting from her family and began to question why she'd tried so hard to get away from them. They did nothing to protect her or help her break the new routine. While no longer funding university costs she now needed money for her substantial heroin addiction, which she continued to fund through sex work back at home. Her mother even helped her with contacts and a 'good' pimp. She was eventually arrested for soliciting.

Maisy hates being a prostitute and presents as a vulnerable young woman of twenty-one. This contrasts with others I've worked with who have adopted a hardened persona to shield themselves from the trauma. Some even describe the pleasure they get from the freedom of being self-employed and doing a job they enjoy. Maisy, meanwhile, recalls every sexual encounter with revulsion.

She's still dozing, so I pat her and ask if she's all right. There's no response, but she is clearly breathing and not in imminent danger. I've finished my paperwork and use the time to look for recipes and inspiration for dinner, wishing I'd bought more than just Maisy's sandwiches this morning. I pat her again, and this time she stirs, then devours the sandwiches and gulps down the water.

'Busy night?' I ask.

'Yeah, I haven't slept yet. Ten, plus the waiting around in between.'

'Good grief – ten different men?'

'Two were only hand jobs though.'

'How much do you charge for that?'

'A fiver.'

'Five pounds?! That's not much.'

'It doesn't take long usually, so I can fit that in while I'm waiting for a proper job.'

'How much do you charge for the whole thing?'

'£15.'

I'm stunned at how little she charges for such a dangerous job. This was in the early 2010s, but a *Daily Mail* article from 2018 reported that prostitutes were still charging as little as £10. I'm slightly nervous about doing a fuller Google search in case the internet thinks I'm seeking a career change.

When I ask her to describe a typical evening, Maisy tells me that she has a shower, gets ready, dressing in a short skirt and top as it's both easy access and means she can remain dressed. She then stands on a street corner, where a couple of other sex workers are also waiting. It doesn't take long for a car to pull up, a hand will point to her and she gets in, quoting the price as she sits in the front seat.

At this point I'm already wondering how she dares get in the car with these strange men. While accurate statistics are hard to come by, one survey found seventy-four per cent of sex workers had been physically assaulted by clients, and half sexually assaulted. Other studies suggest female sex workers are eighteen times more likely to be murdered than the general population.* Maisy agrees that it feels odd at first but, like anything, you get used to it. She says she doesn't get attacked 'that often', but refuses to expand. What upsets her more is being treated like a prostitute when she's not 'on duty' – men recognise her from the street corner and feel entitled to shout abuse at her in the street, and she's also subject to lewd comments from police officers. She said she expects the violence, but always feels shocked and offended by their words.

They drive to a well-known spot on the outskirts of town, where others have also parked to do the same thing, providing a certain sense of security. When it's over, she's driven back. There's no set time limit, but sessions are relatively quick, lasting anything from twenty minutes to an hour, including travel. There is no kissing, cuddling or oral sex (though she'll

---

*   See Stewart Cunningham et al., 'Sex work and occupational homicide: Analysis of a U.K. murder database', *Homicide Studies*, 22(3), 2018.

do that for £50 if she's extra hard up), just 'straight' or a hand job. Hand jobs are conducted in a doorway near where she stands as it's not worth the money to travel.

'Do you enjoy any of it?'

'No, not really. I get the odd one who's okay, I s'pose.'

Changing the subject, I ask about the types of men she's involved with – are there are any cultural differences she's noticed? She smiles and says that now she comes to think of it there are. 'Broadly speaking, Asian men like to barter and try to pay after sex rather than before and then attempt to avoid paying at all. I'm strict with them and make sure they pay up first, no haggling. The price is the price, but once they know the rules, they stick with it, so it's okay.'

'Eastern European men often carry knives, they're rough, there's no chat and they just get on with it. They're good customers because they always pay the correct amount up front, so I don't mind and nobody has ever used the knife, I've just felt it in their pocket. I always do a quick safety feel around their body without them being aware.

'English men turn up in their cars with a child seat in the back. They pay the full price up front. Once the deed is done, they want feedback, ideally compliments, to be told that I'm impressed and that they're the best.'

This makes us both laugh. I wonder if any of them snort in her ear afterwards like Tom does, but I decide not to ask. Maisy is a strikingly pretty girl when she smiles, which sadly isn't very often.

'Have you got a worst one?'

'Yes, definitely. He's called Barry, you might have seen him around town, I think he likes it at the station.'

I get goosebumps. I ask Maisy to describe him and it's clearly a match. Looking into her twenty-one-year-old pixie-like face, with her turned-up nose, green eyes and scruffy hair, I hope I'm not wincing. She's no more than five foot two. The idea of Barry on top of her is horrifying.

Unable to resist asking about the practicalities since I know Barry doesn't have a car, I find out what I didn't really need to know. They do it standing up in a doorway, which is mercifully quick. Trying to force the vision from my mind, I wonder instead about the occupant of the house and how they leave home if Maisy is working in their doorway but decide to keep my mouth shut.

So this is the position she finds herself in. Having sex with several strangers a night to fund her heroin addiction. She has a 'hit' before work to get her through it. Seeing how she looks after her morning hit, I'm shaken to think that these men can have sex with someone so clearly incapacitated.

When I ask Maisy about it, she says, 'It's cuz they like the power and they're all pervy bastards.'

She's probably right.

There are places she could get help, including a charity that will visit sex workers at night and offer support, condoms and a safe place to sit, but she always refuses. 'I'm embarrassed. They seem like nice people, so I don't want to talk to them when I'm at work. I bet they're judging me. Anyway, they're do-gooders that insist on calling us sex workers. I'm a prostitute. I might hate it, but I know what I am.' There are residential organisations where she could go and detox, get intensive counselling and be safe, but so far, she has also turned these down. With the image of Barry fresh in my mind, I resolve to persuade her to go to one of these. Having already tried to get her mentally prepared for this option with little progress, I proffer once again:

'Maisy, you could go to a residential unit. It would be miles away from here. You'd be safe. You could get off the drugs and stop having to work. You could start again.'

She shoots me down with a 'stop going on' look – I recognise it from my children. I promptly abandon the subject for another time.

Until she changes her mind, I'll just have to chaperone her while she sleeps in my office every week, her eyes rolling around in her head before she gains consciousness for a short time and we can actually chat. There are six months left on her Order, just enough time for her to change her mind and for me to get funding for a place so she can get away.

Mick is finally back from his holiday and on his first day in the office he is in early again to see Barry. When I arrive an hour later, rather than looking disgruntled as he usually does on a 'Barry day', he's looking pleased with himself.

'I've organised for Barry to be banned from the railway station. That'll fuck him up and save everyone in there, plus I can have a lie-in once a week.'

Mick looks positively gleeful about his next announcement, telling me that Barry reported that my home visit had provided him a week's worth of wanking. The news makes me wince as I recall the penis on the window, but I hope that I've also inadvertently provided Maisy with a break from him. She's my favourite of the three sex workers I supervise.

Another, forty-year-old Jem, has been 'on the game' for years, using prostitution to fund a truly colossal amphetamine habit. Our sessions could not be any more different to the quiet and subdued appointments I have with Maisy. Jem fidgets and wriggles around in her chair, and can't get her words out fast enough, talking so quickly that she's completely unintelligible. Her shrill voice gets louder each time I ask for clarification. She leaves no opportunity to answer and therefore you can only sit in silence as she rants and raves. Regularly raped and beaten by her boyfriend, who also acts as her pimp and drug supplier, she maintains that she loves him despite bearing fresh injuries every week. Her misshapen nose is only one of the indicators of her most recent beating, along with regular black eyes and bruises around her arms. Her life is a whirlwind of chaos. Her children were taken from her years ago and adopted. She is clearly distraught but could never take the necessary steps to protect them or herself.

She appears regularly in the Magistrates' Court for soliciting, possession of drugs or public nuisance. On occasion, the prosecution, her defence solicitor and I manoeuvre the bench into imposing a custodial sentence, saying that there is no other option, which isn't far from the truth. We can't keep her safe in the community and she flatly refuses to engage with any agencies that could support her, claiming she can't be away from her boyfriend. In prison we know for certain he can't hurt her for a few months and hope she uses the time to come to her senses, but she never does.

The body's almost magical power to heal itself means she is revitalised by the time she is released. The drug-induced acne is gone, and her face reclaims its former clarity. But her boyfriend is always there waiting at the gate for her to come out and by the evening, she is high on speed and, the following day, back to selling her body.

The third sex worker I supervise is Natalie, another woman who should have had a better life, but whose pimp is her own mother, a brothel owner. Natalie constantly steals from her mother to buy drugs, and her mother procures clients for Natalie as a sort of refund. Last time I saw Natalie, it was in prison, where I asked if she had a favourite day in her life. She told me it was the day she appeared on daytime television and was introduced to her birth father for the first time. Her parents had argued and wrestled on the stage. Natalie was delighted that they appeared to be fighting over her. Her father promised in front of hundreds of thousands of television viewers that after all these years he would ensure that he would be a regular part of her life. She let herself dream that he would save her, but she never saw him again. A moment of fame had been his only motivation. Regardless of the harms perpetuated by her own mother, Natalie won't hear a word against her. Natalie visibly transforms in prison from a gaunt, deathly-looking figure into a pretty young woman. Which makes me think of the film *Pretty Woman*, to which prostitution in the real world bears no resemblance. In reality, the girls and women are usually addicts, their clients repulsive, and nobody comes to save them.

It is notable that, like burglars, the prostitutes I work with are drug users trying to fund their habits. But women tend to do this by harming themselves through sex work. While Jem also shoplifts, she views this as a victimless crime – if you don't count the abuse she hurls when she's caught, she doesn't target individuals. Only eight per cent of burglaries are committed solely by women.* Men, in their pursuit of money, tend to take a more destructive route.

***

Keen to ensure Maisy breaks her cycle of drug use and prostitution, I start an application for residential rehab, including applying for funding. She doesn't have a long Probation Order so I must work quickly. When I ask if she agrees, she hesitates before saying yes. She has also accepted a cup of tea from the charity that patrols the red-light area at night, and though it doesn't seem like much, it is a momentous step forward. At least someone else is looking out for her too.

As usual, today Maisy is slumped across my desk, exhausted. She's had another busy night. Many of her customers return on a regular basis, including Barry. Having never told her that I know him, I do my best to hide my look of horror whenever she mentions him.

'I'm nearly used to him now. He's quick and he pays up,' she says.

At a time in her life when she should be experiencing her first enjoyable relationships with men of her own age, being

---

* On average between April 2013 and March 2024. This does not include burglaries committed by both men and women. See 'Nature of crime: burglary, year ending March 2024', Office for National Statistics Centre for Crime and Justice, 8 April 2025: https://www.ons.gov.uk/peoplepopulationandcommunity/crimeandjustice/datasets/natureofcrimeburglary.

'nearly used' to a sex offender captures her near total loss of dignity.

I explain that she won't have to put up with it for much longer and I feel a worrying amount of excitement for her. Her written application to the residential rehabilitation centre (completed by me and signed by her) was successful. She passed the telephone interview (conducted with me there so I could prompt her with answers). We are on the precipice of Maisy being 'saved' only a week before the end of her Probation Order.

She doesn't look as pleased as I'd hoped but I assume this is because she is overwhelmed by all the new possibilities that are opening up for her. Residential placements are like gold dust and they tend to have huge waiting lists. I have quite literally begged for her to have a place. As she listens to my excitement and flicks through the brochure, she seems subdued. With the help of a sex work charity, I've booked and paid for her travel. Her final appointment with me will be at the train station in a few days. To say I am happy for her is an understatement and, as she leaves my office, she gives me a hug and thanks me for all my help. She looks particularly sad but I choose to ignore the sinking feeling in my stomach.

The days pass quickly. After speaking to Maisy on the phone and reminding her of our meeting time, I head for the station to see her off. Arriving early, I notice Barry is outside sitting on his bike watching the people inside the station. He has both of his feet on the ground either side of his bike and is moving backwards and forwards. *Oh my God, he's having a wank.*

The vision of him reaffirms that Maisy has to get out of here. However, after half an hour of waiting, there is no sign of her. I call her again, but she doesn't answer.

Her train comes and goes, and I know that she isn't going to come. After months of pressuring and cajoling her to do what I think is best, I finally recognise my mistake. Never once have I really listened to her, heard what she was saying. Every week, I watched her sleep and then used the little time left to impart advice. She said she doesn't like being a prostitute, but she never told me she wanted to stop, nor did she ever say she wanted to stop using drugs. I've just assumed these things. In my desperation to help, to save her from people like Barry, I've broken the most basic rule of helping anyone. I've imposed my own assumptions.

From years of experience I know that the most effective way to help is to guide and encourage someone's own dreams and desires, not to dictate my own. But this time I failed. Angry at my own stupidity and guilty for letting both Maisy and the rehab centre down, I return to work deflated.

'Don't worry, we've all done it.'

'I'm so pissed off with myself, Mick. It's the last day of her Order, so she doesn't even need to come back, I can't check if she's all right.'

'You can't win them all. Stop being hard on yourself.'

I try calling her again, but she doesn't answer. She has no legal obligation to speak to me now that her Order is over and unless she is made the subject of another one, I'll have no way of finding out how she is. I can only hope that somehow, somewhere, she sorts herself out.

At home that evening, still sad and annoyed with myself, I sit with Tom in the bathroom as he takes a shower. I tell him about my day, hoping my story might elicit some sympathy. Halfway through pouring my heart out and waiting for some comfort from him, I look up to see his penis pressed against the shower door. He hasn't listened to a word I've said. He's probably waiting for me to tell him he's the best.

10

Andrew

It's Saturday. My entire family are coming over to celebrate my parents' fiftieth wedding anniversary. Having promised a buffet (and now wishing I hadn't), I set to work cooking for eighteen people. I feel like Nigella without the equipment, talent or boobs. Or the hourglass figure, the cascade of dark hair, the soft lighting, the stunning kitchen, the organic ingredients… Nevertheless, I'm really enjoying myself creating a mess in the kitchen and have produced a wide range of food and arty cupcakes. Tom remarks that it is a classy spread – there's not a single ham sandwich or cheesy puff. He's impressed and for a moment I wish I could be a housewife full time.

My cousin, a prison officer, has arrived and, having been based in the local prison myself for a couple of years, the conversation soon turns to work. Following the imposition of a custodial sentence, prisoners have mugshots taken, which are kept on the prison database. My cousin and I discuss some of the games played by staff over inmate pictures during break times. It takes too long to leave the prison for lunch, so everyone makes their own fun in the office. The current game of choice is 'spot the nonce'. In my day it was 'who would you shag for a million pounds'. Before you come for me, I hold my hands up at the inappropriateness of these games. My cousin is convinced, however, that sex offenders are the cleanest cut and least dodgy-looking of all the inmates and often twice their age. I concede that he has a point, but we both agree that when it comes to cell cleanliness, it's hard to beat a murderer.

We all enjoy a jolly day drinking too much, so when everyone goes, we decide to leave the tidying up until the morning. Waking up in the middle of the night for the inevitable wee, I can hear rummaging in the kitchen, so I creep downstairs, convinced it's the cat eating leftovers. I'm ready to pounce but instead of a shocked cat, I find a shocked burglar – tall and broad, incongruously adorned in a large array of necklaces, presumably belonging to the neighbours. Speechless, I stare at him.

It's hard to predict how you will react when faced with a burglar in your kitchen. Maybe you'll wrestle them to the ground, overwhelmed by indignant fury or perhaps you'll beg for your life instead, terrified of being stabbed in your own house. I was therefore a bit surprised when, standing in my pyjamas, I heard myself say:

'Hello, Andrew, how are you?'

Just as I stopped short of offering him a cup of tea, he turned tail and struggled back through the kitchen window from whence he came, his top half glowing in the lamplights down the street. Opening my front door – conveniently unlocked, he would have been frustrated to know – I dialled 999 and gave them Andrew's full name, address and date of birth. I'd been supervising him for a few weeks for a shed burglary, clearly not making much of a difference yet.

In view of all the information I'd provided, he was immediately arrested and remanded in custody. I was his sixth house that night. It was an easy cop for the police, and the neighbours got all their jewellery back. Ending up in my kitchen was a spot of bad luck for Andrew, who obviously had no idea that I lived there. He has been prolific for years, using burglary to finance his heroin addiction. In fact, every burglar I see does it to buy drugs, and the drugs in some way embolden them and help them believe that it's okay to go into other people's houses and take things.

Burglary is an engrained part of life for him – a family business that started with his father, also a burglar, also a drug addict. Trained as a child to believe theft was an acceptable way to 'earn' a living, Andrew began by stealing hanging baskets and pot plants from outside houses. He progressed to breaking in himself, his father taking advantage of Andrew's small, child's build to slip through tight spaces and unlock the front door from within. If Andrew didn't meet the goals set by his father, stealing to order, he'd receive a good beating back home. He doesn't feel bitter about this; to him, it was normal. Committing offences was the best way to earn his father's approval.

If he ever has children of his own, he may well teach them to burgle houses and give them a swift smack if they don't do it right. The cycle of social services intervention, arrests, probation and prison will probably continue for another generation. It's important to help him change before that happens.

At thirty-five, Andrew still lives with his parents – except when he steals from them, and they throw him out onto the streets for a few weeks. He eventually returns with his tail between his legs and they let him stay. His regular stints in prison, chaotic lifestyle and drug dependency have denied him any stability. Though tall and sturdily built, his face is gaunt, and his hands thick and swollen – signs of someone who injects anywhere they can find when the veins collapse. He admits that if he can't get heroin, he'll inject anything, from lemonade to cleaning products, just to ease the pain of withdrawal.

Like others with similar backgrounds, by the time Andrew reached adulthood, his behaviour was so entrenched it would have been almost impossible to stop without intervention. There are a number of offending behaviour programmes available in prison and there is evidence to suggest that these really help with a reduction in offending. However, not every prison supplies them and if they do there are long waiting lists to join and therefore many prisoners cannot participate. Without offending behaviour programmes in prisons, being locked up simply doesn't work, with 59.5 per cent of prisoners reoffending following release.[*]

From the comfort of the police car, Andrew points out all the houses he burgled without being caught and these are TIC'd (taken into consideration). He gets brownie points for clearing up open cases by admitting he did it;

---

[*] For recent reoffending rates, see 'Proven reoffending statistics quarterly bulletin, January to March 2023', Ministry of Justice, 30 January 2025: https://assets.publishing.service.gov.uk/media/6793cf91e863a0e7724f4b42/PRSQ_Bulletin_Jan_to_Mar_2023.pdf.

no extra time is added to his sentence, and he can relax in the knowledge that he won't get a surprise arrest later. He's adept at picking locks and creeping around houses at night, but in view of his drug use he can also be sloppy and prone to error. As such, he is an almost permanent fixture in prison, where he gets clean, before relapsing when he's out on licence, committing more burglaries and getting sent back inside.

Andrew chooses to steal jewellery and mobile phones because it's easier to climb out the window with these than with a flat-screen television. He has no awareness that these items might hold personal value to their owners. He's just as happy to steal someone's deceased parents' wedding rings as he is to cause huge inconvenience by stealing people's phones, complete with bank details and thousands of treasured photographs – probably of those same dead parents. He's no different from many other burglars I've worked with, who have little sense of the impact their actions have on victims. Like most, Andrew has a network of people to

---

For more on the role and impact of offending behaviour programmes, see *Prison Education and Accredited Programme Statistics 2023 to 2024*, Ministry of Justice and HM Prison and Probation Service, 26 September 2024; updated 20 November 2024: https://www.gov.uk/government/statistics/prison-education-and-accredited-programme-statistics-2023-to-2024#full-publication-update-history and Ciara Robinson, Annie Sorbie, Johannes Huber, James Teasdale, Katy Scott, Mark Purver and Ian Elliott, *Reoffending impact evaluation of the prison-based RESOLVE Offending Behaviour Programme*, Ministry of Justice, 2021: https://assets.publishing.service.gov.uk/media/601980c8e90e07128d62cd64/RESOLVE_report.pdf.

whom he quickly offloads the stolen items, taking the cash before moving on to the next 'job'.

Burglars come up with all sorts of ways to normalise being in someone else's house and believe it to be perfectly acceptable. Common excuses include:

> 'Nobody was in.'
> 'I didn't hurt anyone.'
> 'I don't go in houses where there are children's toys in the garden.'
> 'I'm not like some burglars. I don't make a mess.'
> 'I've never broken anything.'
> 'It's only stuff, not like I'm beating anybody up!'

Though we work with the full range of other offenders, burglars are often the most challenging to guide to change. With complex needs and issues, it can be hard to know where to start. For people like Andrew, stealing comes as naturally as being messy does to Tom or being a rule-abider does to me. I see my burglars on a Tuesday, just for the petty and childish joy of saying 'CUNextTuesday' – a small pleasure given the extreme frustration of working with them.

For most of us, being in someone else's house when they aren't there feels, well, *weird*. Imagine feeding the fish when your neighbour is on holiday. Letting yourself in, there's a slight sense of discomfort, even though you're doing them a favour. You feed the fish, make sure the heating is off and everything is all right, but don't go in the bedrooms or look in the cupboards, because that's private and the fishbowl is in the living room anyway. Still feeling aware of being in someone's space, you swiftly let yourself out, locking the door behind you.

Burglars have had no such invitation. While some rush in, get the television and any other obvious electronics, then run out again, many go in, have a nose in the drawers, look in the photo albums, go to the loo and have a general browse while deciding what to pinch. In no hurry to leave, some will have a rest and a sit down on the bed, look in the knicker drawer and once they've got everything they fancied taking, stroll off again. As most of them are there to fund a drug habit, they might be off their tits, pausing their search for valuables for a few moments to hallucinate over the floral wallpaper.

It is standard practice for the victims of burglaries to add a few extra items to the list of goods stolen so they can claim more from the insurance company. Notably, this is often equivalent to the insurance excess amount. I know this because when the burglar is in court, the indictment has a list of the goods taken, which the burglar will go through with a fine-tooth comb, ticking off what they actually did steal and complaining about any additions placed there by the victim. At which point they bitterly and indignantly accuse the victim of being a liar and a 'cheating bastard'. They have absolutely no concept of the irony.

As anticipated, Andrew is given another custodial sentence of three years, for the burglary of my house and a few others up the street. Given I'm now one of his victims it would be a conflict of interest for me to continue to see him and he will be transferred to someone else in the team.

A few days later, a letter is waiting on my desk in a familiar prison envelope.

Dear Liz

I never new it was your house, I hope you werent scard. I didn't nick anything at yours as I didn't have time. You looked shocked to see me I can tell you. Ha ha. I don't mind if you carry on being my Probation Officer, I'm fed up with seeing different people every time and we only just getting to know each other, so I'd rather just stick with you then I can tell you Im sorry

Yours Sinceerly
Andrew

It's a short letter, but a big gesture. It's not easy to apologise for something that he has historically felt no remorse about. As far as I know, it's the first time Andrew has ever regretted his crimes. Maybe because he connected the house and its belongings to a human being – someone he actually knew. I know how powerful restorative justice can be, especially when offenders meet their victims, and it has been a useful tool with burglars. While it's highly unusual, I check with my line manager to see if I can keep him. He's been supervised by everyone else in the team over the years, so I was to be his last chance. None of the others want him back, so my manager agrees. I wasn't particularly fazed when I found him in my kitchen, and since we're short-staffed, I'm fairly sure they're saying yes because it's easier than finding someone else.

Andrew appears to have gained nothing from his stints behind bars. The main purpose of prison is containment, not change, rehabilitation or reform. While education is on offer in all prisons, inmates often only take it up because they're bored and don't fully engage, probably due to having felt humiliated or inadequate at school. But another form of education is available to all inmates: how to make weapons out of razor blades, how to avoid getting caught next time and how to 'look after themselves'. Prisoners make up a separate community altogether, a community that can be sidelined and forgotten by the outside world. They are not seen as valuable citizens and so they don't behave as such.

Since offending behaviour programmes are not always available, many prisoners are released having learned nothing that could help them reintegrate into society and as a result they fall into the same situation they were in before they went inside, if not a worse one. Andrew is not unusual in having adopted crime as a way of life and reverting to what is familiar is perfectly natural. Every time he is released, he quickly returns to old habits. Meeting a victim – i.e. me – who will work with him without judgement might present the opportunity he needs to change, particularly as his letter demonstrated *some* regret.

I visit him in prison. Andrew doesn't look embarrassed at all; instead, he gives me a cheeky smile.

'Sorry, Miss.'

'Miss' is the standard term for any female visitor in prison, and it's shouted so often across the landings that all women present answer to it.

'Call me Liz.'

'All right, Miss.'

'Andrew, tell me how you felt meeting the resident of the house.'

'I thought, "Fuck, how am I going to get out of here?" But I also thought, "This is where somebody lives, it's not just empty." I always burgle at night. I'm careful, quiet. I do what I have to do and leave. All I think about the people living there is: they have so much more than I do. It's not fair, in their nice houses with all their stuff. If they've got photographs on the wall, I'll have a quick look. They look pleased with themselves. They're on holiday. I've never had a holiday. I take what I need and leave. They're insured anyway, so what's the problem? They'll get the money back. I did feel a bit bad when I saw you, though, Miss. Oh my God, your face. Your kitchen is a right mess. I felt sorry for you before I even knew who it was.'

Andrew starts cackling, and we laugh together for a few moments at the thought of my messy kitchen.

Changing the subject, I ask, 'Are you happy, Andrew?'

'What, in this shithole?'

When someone has such entrenched behaviour and views, it is vital not to tell them off or make judgements. Changing is a frightening process. It's hard to give up everything you've ever known, to reinvent yourself. I know to tread carefully with him.

'Describe a time when you've been happy.'

Andrew is quiet.

'I feel happy when I score [heroin] but that's relief rather than happiness. But when it starts working, I feel excited, like being in heaven, warm, like I'm wrapped up in cotton wool. The colours are brighter, everything looks beautiful. I feel like I can take on the world, but when it wears off again, I feel like shit. My body hurts and shivers. It's freezing cold.

I'm angry and would do anything to feel good again. I know it's not happiness. I don't know what that is. That's why it's all right in prison. It usually takes a few days before the medical team come with a methadone script [prescription], so it makes you scream in agony while you're rattling [withdrawing] but loads of other people in the prison are doing the same, so that helps. I know loads of people in here, I've got mates who understand me, even the screws. This time I've just done the rattle, so I'm straight. It's all right.' He pauses. 'Nobody has ever asked me if I'm happy before.'

I ask him to go back to the beginning. We talk about his childhood shoplifting, how he got the rush of adrenaline running into shops and stealing things before dashing out to his waiting father, who would be delighted. He enjoyed the time he spent with his dad but also felt the pressure of getting more and more. He was good at it.

'I've always been tidy. I don't make a mess like my dad. It's disrespectful.'

Andrew tells me about school, how he didn't have any friends. He wasn't invited to anyone's house because he had a reputation for stealing. He was always in trouble; the teachers didn't like him. Nobody expected anything from him. Andrew played to type, leaving school with no qualifications or prospects of finding work.

'Do you really want to keep coming back to prison? You're worth more than that.'

'Not really, but what else am I going to do?'

I remind him that he's not just a burglar, that he's also a likeable man with good attention to detail. I tell him how his excellent memory has been noted as he remembers the addresses of every burglary he's done and has never missed a probation appointment, despite often being under the influence of drugs, which contrasts with many others who can't recall what day it is.

Early on in his 'career' he was assessed by a psychiatrist who determined he had learning difficulties. This 'fact' has followed him around in his file ever since and been cited as one of the reasons for his offending. Wondering if it's time for a new assessment, I ask him if he would be prepared to undertake some psychometric and ability testing with our employment officer, Pauline. He'll be serving eighteen months in prison – maybe he could use the time to work towards something.

He complies and takes the tests, which show he has above average skills in verbal, spatial and non-verbal abilities, but his numerical scores are incredibly high. Pauline presents him with a certificate, the first he has ever had. She reports that he immediately held himself differently. He tells her he'd like to do a GCSE in Maths. Being rid of the shackles of his previous assessment has given him the confidence to try. He also announces that as he's gone through the 'rattle' anyway, he's decided not to accept the methadone prescription. He wants to be clean of drugs when he comes out. He starts to associate with the inmates he meets in the maths class and tries to stay away from his usual prison friends while maintaining his 'hard man' prison swagger so that he's left alone. His eagerness to learn replaces his desire to be the hardest, the most dishonest and the most likely to be back in prison.

Andrew gets an A in his GCSE and is elated. Three months before being freed, he starts to worry about returning to his parents' house and falling into old habits. The Probation Service's accommodation officer goes to see him and reserves a bedsit for him and a place on the council waiting list. Meanwhile Pauline, the employment officer, has contacts with many local businesses and has secured an interview with one of them for him upon his release. For the first time he's excited about his liberty, and has hope for his future. He has a team of people around him who have some belief in him and have offered encouragement and support. The prison officers who usually expect him to be straight back inside have started to believe in him too, their attitudes towards him morphing into something like respect.

The hardest part of a prison sentence is coming out. In fact, one of my clients was so tormented about his release that he hanged himself the day he was due to come out, the prison officer unable to resuscitate him. While there's the anticipation of being free, there is also fear. There are so many obstacles in the way of reform: finding somewhere to live, getting a job, getting to know people who aren't going to lead you astray. The stigma of being an ex-offender means finding decent accommodation and employment is very difficult, leading offenders to conclude that they don't belong in society, so they'll stick with what they know and go back to crime. After all, as many of them bemoan, 'What has anyone ever done for me?'

If Andrew is to prosper, we need to foster a support network. He is referred to a drug recovery service which can help him stay off drugs and provide regular drug tests to prove he hasn't relapsed. Pauline assists with job applications. Though Andrew doesn't have any previous employment experience, he does now have a GCSE and together they are able to highlight his strengths, including his resilience and his ongoing determination to stay sober. He has distanced himself from his father and old friends, which has been a huge emotional wrench. She negotiates with a local employer, who takes a chance on him in his garage and gives him an apprenticeship.

Dressed in a scruffy grey hoodie and stretchy joggers that rest on his hips revealing the label of his underwear and the crack of his arse, Andrew looks like a criminal. I encourage him to change his image before starting work, and after applying to some charities, we go shopping. I'm unprepared for how vulnerable he seems coming out of the changing room in well-fitted trousers, asking if he looks a twat. He's transformed into someone completely new. He's scared about his new life but also excited by its potential. Despite his reputation as a hard nut, a lifelong burglar and drug addict, Andrew is actually a softie. He wants to succeed and to be part of the community.

After a few months living in the bedsit and working at the garage Andrew is allocated a flat by the local council. The flat is entirely empty. He has nothing. Despite being well into his thirties, he has never lived fully independently before. I've found a few old things around our house – old curtains and such – that I've given him, and I've asked friends if they have any spare household items. My friend Sam has just bought new furniture and has agreed to give Andrew her old stuff. It's still in good condition and includes a bed. Incidentally, she's married to a policeman, Bob, and we deliver the furniture to Andrew one evening. Andrew is very emotional, telling Bob he's never experienced kindness from a policeman before. Similarly, Bob had never met a burglar outside a police station and is surprised by this friendly and charming man and genuinely wishes him well.

Installed in his new flat, Andrew feels ready for love and proudly announces during our supervision session that he has a date. His first in three years. He hopes that afterwards he can take her home to see his flat, complete with new furniture. Excited too, I can barely wait until next week to find out how he gets on.

A week later, Andrew is *very* upset. After years of abstinence, instead of it being as romantic as he'd hoped, he'd had a very disappointing evening.

'I've been used. She was just intrigued to see what it was like to have sex with someone who hadn't done it in years. As soon as the deed was done, she got up and left. And to top it off, I bought her dinner, and she gave me crabs. I have sex once, then have to spend the day in the clap clinic scratching.'

'Oh no! Are you all right?'

'I'll live. I can't believe I fell for that, now I know how women feel. I've boil-washed my new sheets. I'm becoming a dab hand at washing, plus now I'm not stealing, my mum has been coming to visit. She's well impressed with my washing skills. Maybe it's good I haven't got a woman yet, I'm just getting to know my mum again. She's well proud of me. A flat, a job. Who'd have thought it?'

Pauline goes to see Andrew's boss, who raves about his new apprentice, but one day I get a call from the drug support agency. Andrew has had a positive drugs test. After all this, I can't help but feel deflated. I could have him recalled as he is still on licence with conditions not to use drugs, but wait until he comes in. Before I even ask, he blurts out that he saw his old friends and couldn't resist trying heroin again with them. My disappointment in him is nothing compared to his own. He is furious with himself. Recalling him would put him straight back to his old habits again. He would lose his job and flat, so I give him the benefit of the doubt and drug test him again myself. He's clean this time. Being allowed to make one mistake without dismantling everything he's built is a powerful lesson. He is acutely embarrassed and recommits, determined not to slip up again. Instead of dobbing him in, we just talk about it instead.

Society is often fixated on comeuppance rather than redemption. But I have seen that through forgiveness, people can change. As Andrew likes to remind me, he pays taxes now, contributing to society rather than taking from it. He has too much to lose to make another mistake – and he doesn't.

At his final appointment, Andrew looks overcome. He's nervous about being without the support he's grown used to but also pleased that he has come to the end with a job, the backing of his boss, new friends, and a more positive relationship with his mum. He gives me a thank-you card and some chocolates. We're not allowed to accept gifts, so I pass them along to the reception team and, after eating a few on the way, I feel optimistic about his future.

**

In 2014, 'Through the Gate', a study exploring the impact of support provided to prisoners during the transition from prison to probation, was published. It showed that when Probation Officers build a rapport and provide practical support – such as connecting offenders to housing, employment services and mental health care – this support system significantly reduces the likelihood of reoffending. Offenders who feel they are treated with dignity and have a positive relationship with their Probation Officers are more likely to successfully reintegrate into society.

Similarly, *Research on Probation Trusts* (published in 2010) found that Probation Officers who take a more enabling approach to supervision and offer support, guidance and practical help are more successful at reducing reoffending compared to those who adopt a punitive approach. The 2011 study *UK Probation Research on Motivational Interviewing* demonstrated how the use of motivational interviewing (MI) in probation has been shown to reduce reoffending. MI focuses on building relationships based on empathy and support, which helps offenders make positive changes. Research indicates that Probation Officers who use MI techniques effectively can build trust and improve the chances of offenders adhering to their rehabilitation plans.

The UK's 'What Works' initiative (2000s–2010s) in probation services focused on evidence-based practices for reducing reoffending. One key element of 'What Works' is the quality of supervision and the relationship between the officer and the offender. Studies within this framework have shown that positive, rehabilitative relationships lead to better outcomes in terms of reduced recidivism, as they encourage offenders to actively engage in treatment and rehabilitation programmes.

This research in the UK aligns with international findings that a positive relationship with Probation Officers is a key factor in reducing reoffending. Studies from various sources – government reports, probation trusts and offender management systems – indicate that when Probation Officers treat offenders with respect, empathy and support, and when they focus on building trust, offenders are more likely to engage in rehabilitation and have lower chances of reoffending.

To avoid being burgled yourself, here's some tips I've learned along the way:

1. **Leave toys in the front garden.** Burglars with a conscience avoid houses with children.
2. **Install a camera**, even if it's a pretend one, with a big notice saying, 'I've got a camera'.
3. **Don't leave windows open.**
4. **Have a noisy driveway** with pebbles on that alert you to intruders.
5. **Put up a 'Beware of the Dog' sign**, although if you've got a valuable dog who will go for a walk with anyone, they might pinch that too.
6. **If you've got a nice car, hide the keys.** Some burglars steal cars to order. I leave the keys in the ignition, but that's because my car is too crap for anyone to take.
7. **If you've been burgled they are more likely to come back** because they know where everything is. Change the locks and do all of the above.

8. **Have a burglar alarm** – a conspicuous pretend one will do.
9. **Most burglars I've met are lazy** and steal from the local area. If you live near a burglar, move.

Clearly, I ignored all of the above, which is why Andrew broke in.

11

Luke

It's Saturday and I've been perched on a hard chair in the kitchen for an hour with my head covered in ripped up bits of tin foil, getting highlights. Tom is patiently modelling for our son Josh, who is artfully covering up his bald patch and trimming the sides. Amazingly, it doesn't look like a combover. Josh has a gift! We have agreed to be Josh's guinea pigs while he trains as a hairdresser and it's become a nice opportunity for us to spend time together and talk idly about our weeks. Inevitably, they ask if I've had any 'funny' clients this week, so I tell them about 'Barry the Wanker'.

Maybe, deep down, I'm looking for respect or sympathy. I wonder if they are proud of me for going to a sex offender's house on my own without back-up. Or if they have a view on the system which allows – well, facilitates – that. But they've heard so many of my stories at this point, I can't quite manage to hold their attention. I used to think women were ignored at home because they were talking 'domestics', which their husbands, engaged in real world problems through 'serious' jobs, found dull. But if *my* job doesn't entertain or interest them, there's not a lot more I can do.

Josh changes the subject back to hair after I mention the peroxide is burning my scalp. Post-rinse, the result is so uneven I start to calculate how long before I can show myself in public again. But because Josh is my son and I love him, I tell him it's perfect. I detect a flash of horror in his eyes when he looks at me, before he hurriedly announces he needs to change for the pub.

Later, he struts downstairs looking like a pop star. 'Don't get into any fights!' I can't help saying as he heads to the front door.

'Give over, Mum, stop going on.'

'Just be careful.'

I worry every time he goes out. I know that at twenty years old he's in the group that has the highest chance of being attacked in the street.*

'The most common injury is a black eye, you don't want anyone to ruin your face, do you? Keep your head down and keep away from people.'

Looking out of the window, I watch him disappear down the road.

***

Across town, Sally is enjoying an unusual weekend off from her job as a nurse, spending it with her twenty-year-old son

---

* *The nature of violent crime in England and Wales: year ending March 2024*, Office for National Statistics, 26 September 2024: https://www.ons.gov.uk/peoplepopulationandcommunity/crime andjustice/articles/thenatureofviolentcrimeinenglandandwales/ yearendingmarch2024.

Scott. Sally wants to treat him and has made his favourite dinner of fish fingers, chips and peas. She's bought him some new clothes and he is putting handfuls of products into his newly cut hair. He smiles at his reflection. *Hench*, he thinks.

'Scott, you look so handsome, are you out to impress someone?'

'Mum, stop going on!'

'Do you still like that girl, Ellie? Has she dumped that other lad, Luke yet? I can see you're making a big effort today.' She waits for an answer.

'They split up last week. I'm hoping to see her out tonight.'

Sally smiles. As Scott leaves the house, she's by the door. She insists on giving him a hug.

He pushes her away: 'Get off, Mum!'

'Be careful. Don't get into any fights.'

'I'm a lover not a fighter,' Scott replies, laughing. He disappears down the road with a bounce in his step. He's liked Ellie for years.

***

Round the corner, Luke is also ready to go out. He and his mum, Carol, and his dad, Ray, are chatting.

'Do you think you and Ellie will get back together?'

'Of course we will, Mum. She loves me.'

'You look *very* handsome, Luke. Doesn't he Ray? She won't be able to resist you!'

Luke's been hitting the gym and it shows. He peeks at his six pack in the mirror, feeling pleased with himself. He's had his hair cut; an apprentice called Josh did it – a decent job too. He runs his fingers through it and stands back from his reflection.

'You could be a contestant on *Love Island*!'

'Mum, for God's sake.'

'You're so handsome, I'm sure Ellie will come running back.'

'I'm off now, Mum, bye…'

'Love you! Have a great night and be careful – there's some weird people out there.'

'Mum, I'll be fine!'

He shuts the door behind him. Carol and Ray watch him disappear down the road. They feel proud. At nineteen, he's in his second year of a carpentry apprenticeship, with top marks so far. He's always been creative and he's usually such a happy lad, but he's been in a mood all week after his argument with Ellie. He'll soon forget her. He's young and there's plenty of other girls.

***

Josh sticks his head through the door at the Golden Fleece. It's packed. He spots Luke, whose hair he cut today, chatting to a girl by the bar. *Did a good job of that one*, he notes as he scans the pub for his friends. No one's there, so off he heads to the Red Lion.

Back at the Golden Fleece, Luke is trying to make conversation with Ellie, but she's not interested. Scott is staring at her longingly from the other side of the room, hoping for his chance to go over to her. He's pleased. He can see that she's not interested in Luke. *Their relationship is definitely over*, he thinks to himself. Luke turns from the bar disgruntled and sits with his mates. He downs his pint in one and returns to the bar for more. Ellie has retreated to another table with her friends. Scott keeps an eye on her, waiting for an opportunity to go and say hello. He's oblivious to his friends laughing and talking around him, nor has he noticed that Luke is now staring at him staring at Ellie.

Luke finishes his next pint and lurches to the bar for another. His friend shouts 'slow down' after him. Luke ignores him and buys another. His face is red and blotchy, a mixture of alcohol and anger. Meanwhile Scott sees his chance to talk to Ellie – her friends have gone to the bar, and she's sitting on her own.

'You okay, Ellie?'

'Yes, good thanks, are you?'

Luke suddenly appears.

'Are you chatting my girlfriend up?'

'She's not your girlfriend anymore, mate,' replies Scott.

'Are you trying to humiliate me in front of her?'

Ellie interrupts: 'Come on now, Luke. He's literally only said hello.'

Luke is visibly agitated and starts raving about how he's been watching Scott stare at Ellie before shoving him. Scott stumbles, knocking over some glasses before steadying himself. The landlord comes over and orders them to take their argument outside. Scott agrees: 'Come on, let's just have a chat, mate, get some air while you calm down.'

In the street Luke snarls at Scott. 'Don't you look fucking smug at me.' He considers that Scott might be good-looking, maybe more than him. Maybe Ellie does like him. Blind with anger and barely thinking, Luke punches Scott in the side of his face. It feels good. He watches Scott fall backwards and hit his head on the kerb. Scott tries to get up, but instead stares directly into Luke's face, dazed. He's scared, Luke can see it. For a brief moment Luke feels vindicated, but it quickly gives way again to rage. How dare he try to get up. Before Scott is even upright, he kicks him in the side of his head.

Falling to the ground, Scott feels a kick in his back, then another, then another. The first one hurt, but the rest don't. He can hear thuds, but he can't feel them. Looking at the curb, he knows he's on the ground, but he doesn't know what that thudding sound is.

Luke is so full of rage he can't control himself. He's kicking and kicking. *How dare that bastard chat up his girlfriend. Who the fuck does he think he is? Look at him, he's pathetic, lying on the floor.* People are coming out of the pub, panicked, whispering to each other. Luke stops kicking. He can't be bothered to talk to any of them. 'Fuck the lot of you!' he growls. He turns towards home, and finds himself running, the speed fills him with elation, but it can't block out the sickness swelling in his stomach.

Back outside the pub, Ellie is stroking Scott's hair, she can feel the grease from the products mingled with the sticky warmth of blood between her fingers. She strokes and strokes – maybe if she keeps stroking, he'll wake up. Other people are standing around, someone is screaming, there are shouts to call an ambulance. It's a warm evening, but the landlord comes over and puts a blanket over Scott, who is motionless on the floor. Someone is kneeling beside him, their ear to his nose, feeling for a pulse. There's the sound of crying. Scott's friends are calling for Luke's address: 'I'm going to find him and fucking kill him.' They're pacing, chests puffed, agitated and looking for a fight, with absolutely no sense of the irony.

Scott is surrounded by people. Ambulance staff and police officers push them aside, barking instructions, asking for details. They take him away in an ambulance.

'I'll come with him,' says Ellie, 'I'm his girlfriend.' She doesn't know why she says it. She's liked him since school. She wants – wanted – to be his girlfriend.

Luke arrives home, breathless.

'You're home early, Luke.'

'Yeah Mum, had too much to drink.' He vomits in the toilet before crawling into bed. It's only 9 o'clock.

***

Sally is at home watching *Strictly Come Dancing*. It's particularly good today. She wonders if Scott has been confident enough to talk to Ellie.

***

One of the first things I notice is how immaculate Luke's tiny cell is. The light is shining from the small, barred window on to photographs of his mum and dad, the family dog, a not-so-long-ago holiday. They are all smiling. There's a picture of Luke with a protective arm around his younger brother, both sporting tans on a faraway beach. The photos are tacked to the wall at right angles. More pictures around his bed of friends, all smiling. Luke in the middle. The bed is perfectly made like he's in the army – nobody would guess a twenty-year-old boy lived here.

It's my first meeting with Luke; he is on remand and due for sentencing in a few weeks. I'm preparing his Pre-Sentence Report as the court want to know why a young man with no previous convictions could have killed someone. I'm researching all I can about him. He's already been in prison for nearly a year and has acquired the ashen complexion of most inmates – the face of someone who hasn't been outside much in months. He appears surprisingly nonchalant considering the circumstances. When I ask how he's getting on, he replies: 'It's all right, Miss, I've made some friends. LOADS of women write to me. Look.' He brandishes a pile of letters proudly. 'I spend a lot of time replying to them. I've been reading a lot and college have sent me books so I can carry on studying. Obviously, I can't use a saw though!' He's pleased with the joke and I note how he's slipped into using prison lingo.

He doesn't share the gentle accent of his parents, who I met yesterday. They live in a comfortable house, full of books. As I sat in their kitchen, mug of tea in hand, their sloppy spaniel sat on my feet. I started fussing him and we compared dogs to break the ice. It reminded me of my own kitchen. His mother expressed relief that someone was finally talking to them. They didn't understand court processes or language and, prior to visiting Luke, they'd never set foot in a prison. They were unsure what was happening. They couldn't understand the charges: why murder not manslaughter?* Nobody had explained anything, and they were struggling to get any information out of Luke. His mum started crying and told me she'd been so nervous about my visit she'd been unable to sleep. The whites of his father's eyes were red with worry and his hands were gently trembling; he caught me looking and hid them in his pockets.

I asked them to describe Luke, the kind of son he'd been. They were visibly relieved to talk about him, the son they had before that terrible night. They described his sense of humour, the practical jokes that made the whole family laugh. His closeness to his younger brother and how he looked out for him. They talked about his love of sports, how he started going out with Ellie, his first girlfriend, when he was seventeen, how they were inseparable; how he'd become moody and sullen after they broke up.

They questioned every aspect of their parenting, as much to themselves as me: 'Did we do something wrong? Was it all the sport we encouraged him to do? Did we put too much pressure on him? Did we expect too much? Were we too lenient? Is it our fault? We still love him, is that all right? What happened to him? Why did our beautiful son do this?'

They wanted to know all about Scott: his parents, what job he did. I told them how Scott was a health care assistant at the local hospital and that he lived with his mum Sally, his dad having left years before. They wanted to know more

---

* Manslaughter is where there is no specific intent to cause harm, for example when a drunk driver kills a pedestrian or a patient dies due to a doctor's gross negligence. While Luke didn't intend to kill Scott, he did intend to hurt him, hence murder.

about Sally. How had it affected her? How was she? I am honest, relaying what Sally told Victims Support, the devastation she felt, the emptiness of her life, the counselling she was receiving, which wasn't helping. Luke's parents felt entirely responsible. His mum kept repeating how sorry she was, sobbing uncontrollably.

It was striking how lovely they were, how ordinary. How do you grapple with the new and shocking reality that you are the parents of a murderer? It's near impossible to imagine. I explain to them that I've already been in touch with Luke's school and college and that Luke had been universally well liked, with no signs of violence. The incident was a shock to everyone who knew him, not just them. It wasn't their fault.

***

Sitting across from Luke in his cell, I ask him what happened. 'I've read everything, witness statements, police reports and your original interview with the police. I see you went "no comment". You've been found guilty now, so it's your opportunity to tell your version for the court.'

Luke takes a sharp intake of breath before talking.

'I'd been going out with Ellie for about two years, I met her at the rowing club. Things were good. I thought we could be together forever, but she had got distant, like she'd already moved on. I knew it was over. I asked her if there was someone else and she said no. I think she'd just got bored with me, but I couldn't help but check around to see if she was telling the truth. Then I saw that Scott bloke in the pub. He was staring at Ellie, she hadn't noticed him, but I had. He was waiting to make a move. I thought if I got pissed, I wouldn't mind, but I got angrier. Scott went over and talked to Ellie. I could see she was pleased, and I felt jealous. I've never felt jealousy before, it was horrible, it grew in the pit of my stomach.

'I went over so he would stop talking to her. I shoved him and the landlord told us to go outside. Scott smiled at me about to say something, but I didn't want to hear him out. I think he wanted to be nice, but it made it worse, he just looked smug. I saw the "red mist", so I punched him, I didn't even know what I was doing, it was like I'd lost control of my mind, it didn't even feel like me anymore, it felt like I was going to explode, I couldn't think. He fell over and hit his head on the kerb. That's what killed him, it wasn't me. It's not fair I'm in here. I could have understood if I got charged with GBH or manslaughter but not murder. I didn't kill him, it was the kerb. He shouldn't have been coming on to Ellie anyway. It was his fault, not mine, he was asking for it.'

I'm distracted by the memory of the post-mortem pictures. The marks on the back of Scott's head from the kerb, the bruises on his face and back from being kicked, his brain, pink and healthy on one side, purple and spongey on the other. I'd been mesmerised by the contents of his stomach. Scott hadn't lived long enough after his dinner to digest his mum's fish fingers and peas.

'I've seen the medical report, Luke, and it was the kicks that killed him. One witness says you were in a frenzy of kicking. Have you ever seen the "red mist" before?'

I wait.

'What do you feel about it?'

More waiting.

'Do you feel guilty, remorseful?'

'Nah, never seen the red mist before. I've never been that angry. I feel bad.'

Dismayed by the understatement, I press him again.

'It wasn't my fault.'

He's gone on the defensive, he's about to shut down and stop talking – I can see it in his face. I leave, promising to return in a few days.

Luke's parents were shocked by his detachment from the magnitude of his actions. They describe how they seemed to feel more guilty than he did. Their sentiments check with my interview. Luke also suggested to them that Scott bears some liability for his own fate, that it wasn't totally Luke's fault. No matter which way he is asked, he resists accepting full responsibility, repeating it was the kerb, not him. After collecting the papers in his file, I turn to leave – he is already cleaning his cell.

Luke's mum calls to see how the visit went. 'Did he always have a tidy bedroom?' I ask her. She's obviously surprised by my question, but answers: 'It was always a tip.'

Luke is sentenced to fifteen years for the murder of Scott. After he is taken away, his parents and Sally hug in the court waiting room. They have all lost a son. I am struck by the grace and bravery of these parents who have sat through all the court hearings; some of the most heart-wrenching and stressful days of their lives, not invited to participate, to vouch for their boys, only admitted as spectators.

LUKE

Sadly, this isn't as unusual as it may sound. Over the years, I have seen many young men like Luke, angry and disinhibited by alcohol. They want to fight, with no thought for the consequences, their victims badly injured or worse. We as a society bear some blame for this. We encourage boys to buckle up, to associate vulnerability with weakness; it is hardly surprising they find it hard to regulate emotions. I don't need to mention the harms of the internet, the toxicity of the manosphere and lack of understanding of what it means to be a young person in a world more polarised than ever before. They aren't encouraged to talk openly about their feelings and the pressure to conform to certain masculine ideals, at the expense of healthier character development, can manifest itself as anger or violence. If Luke had felt comfortable enough to talk openly with his friends without fear of humiliation, he might have described how hurt he was feeling about Ellie rather than bottling it up and resorting to violence. Silently, I thank the Lord that I've encouraged Josh to be so in touch with his emotions that he never stops talking. That, and he went to a different pub on the night of Scott's murder.

I consider Scott and Luke's parents. Sally lost her job as she doesn't have the capacity to help other people anymore. She describes how many friends, after their initial support, drifted away, unable to cope with her continued anguish. She is in regular contact with SAMM (Support after Murder and Manslaughter) but feels unable to move on. Luke's parents, guilty and embarrassed, concerned about their younger children, moved to another part of the country.

I still see Luke, who has finally accepted full responsibility for Scott's death. He notes that it was much easier when he blamed the kerb, but he wanted to face what he had done and so is one of the paltry four per cent of prisoners who seek counselling.* It is vital for him to go through this, to properly process what he has done, so that he can one day re-enter society. Counselling is helping Luke put an end to the constant thoughts of Scott's head hitting the kerb, and make sense of things. Luke is a genuinely nice young man and always was. He had a 'normal' and stable upbringing and made the ultimate mistake in a split second of madness. There was nothing in his past to raise suspicions about his safety – he had never been violent with Ellie and hadn't previously been in fights. He will now spend at least eight years in prison and the rest of his life on licence.

Unable to cope with Scott's death, Sally went to Luke for answers. She contacted the prison and through prison probation, the Restorative Justice scheme, and with Luke's permission, we were able to organise it for her. The Restorative Justice Scheme is entirely voluntary and allows victims and perpetrators to exchange letters or talk to each other in person with the support of fully trained specialist facilitators. While evidence suggests that restorative justice is helpful (eighty-five per cent of victims were pleased they did it), only 4.2 per cent

---

* *Experiences of men who access NHS Talking Therapies from prison: 1 April 2018 to 31 March 2020*, Office for National Statistics, 26 April 2023: https://www.ons.gov.uk/peoplepopulationandcommunity/healthandsocialcare/mentalhealth/articles/experiencesofmenwhoaccessnhstalkingtherapiesfromprison/1april2018to31march2020.

of victims are offered it.* Had Sally not suggested it herself, it is unlikely she would ever have been offered it.

Restorative Justice can be a surprisingly powerful and cathartic journey for both perpetrator and victim. There are well-documented accounts of murder victims' families meeting the perpetrator. These meetings are carefully managed, and the victim's family can ask the questions they've been wanting to, which helps to alleviate the constant imagined scenarios. In some cases, there has been forgiveness and even friendship, a powerful balm in the process of healing.

Sally was taken aback by how ordinary Luke was, nothing like the monster she'd envisioned. Their meeting had commenced with the usual greetings, asking each other how they were, shaking of hands. She couldn't believe that she had touched him, the man who had killed her son. She came to feel sorry for him. After their meeting, the sadness remained, but the gnawing pain caused by the constant questions in her mind were eased. His sincere remorse gave Sally some peace. They talked about Scott. She'd enjoyed talking about her son – he and Luke could have been friends. She also realised through the meeting that Luke was being punished and not experiencing a 'holiday camp'. Luke said that the meeting was the hardest thing he'd ever done in his life but

---

* *Restorative justice, year ending March 2011 to year ending March 2019: Crime Survey for England and Wales (CSEW)*, Office for National Statistics, 18 July 2019: https://www.ons.gov.uk/people populationandcommunity/crimeandjustice/adhocs/010238re storativejusticeyearendingmarch2011toyearendingmarch2019crimes urveyforenglandandwalescsew.

that he was grateful for the chance to say he was sorry. Both spoke positively about their meeting and plan to see each other again.

***

Josh has finished his training. My scalp no longer burns and my hair isn't stripy. It's Saturday, and we are chatting in our usual spots in the kitchen, though this time we are joined by two Spanish exchange students. Much to everyone's irritation, I have countered my paranoia about my children getting into fights by inviting people to stay with us, hoping it will help my children become more tolerant. We are currently trying to entertain two bored eighteen-year-olds. They've had a haircut, which amused them for a few minutes. They don't speak English, so we are communicating via Google translate. They say they have dogs at home in Spain and, pleased we finally have some common ground, we suggest we all go for a walk with Max the dog in the local countryside.

Max, a slow old boy who has never chased anything in his life, unusually goes running off and catches a rabbit. Tom, Josh and I frantically try to get the rabbit off him while our visitors stare at us in slack-jawed horror. Tom eventually grabs Max around the mouth and pulls his mouth open. The rabbit makes good its escape, hotly pursued by the Spanish lads who catch it again. Tom then grapples with them to retrieve the rabbit and save it. He thinks he is fluent in Spanish because he went on holiday to Brazil for a month twenty years ago and is shouting instructions at the Spanish lads in Portuguese. Our guests look perplexed. Tom obviously thinks they are stupid – 'Portuguese is nearly the same as Spanish!' They can't understand a word he's saying. It's likely he's saying it wrong in Portuguese anyway. He finally manages to wrestle the poor rabbit off our visitors, and it runs off unharmed.

We carry on walking, the Spaniards conversing in Spanish and Tom and Josh moaning about me inviting exchange students to stay. Back in our kitchen and with the help of Google translate again, we discover that they use their dogs at home to help them catch rabbits to eat and they think we are foolish for forgoing a delicious rabbit stew. I wonder if they might just be starving. Despite my terrible kitchen skills, I admit I exaggerated on the application form, claiming to be a professional cook.

Monday comes around too quickly. After making breakfast for my family and two hungry Spanish teenagers, I clean up, put the washing out and go to work, marvelling at how my paranoia about Josh getting into a fight has translated into a houseful of Spaniards.

12

Lenny

'Come on girls, get out of the pool. Hurry up – that's it – time to finish!'

Francis' wife glares at him, irritated: 'For fuck's sake, Francis. Not again.'

'Yes, but look at *him*. Why is that man on his own in the kids' swimming pool?'

'He's learning to swim! What is wrong with you?'

'I don't want him looking at our girls. I bet his trunks have "slipped down" under the water.'

'Oh Francis. He's just trying to doggy paddle in shallow water.'

'That's *not* doggy paddle, nobody splashes about like that…'

Francis is in the staff room, regaling us with his weekend. He's in trouble for ruining his daughters' day out… again.

'You just see things *differently* when you work with sex offenders.' We all understand what he means. Out of my current caseload of fifty-six, ten are sex offenders of various sorts that I must see on a weekly basis. There are rapists, paedophiles, internet sex offenders… a man who shags chickens – we see them all. And now I imagine them everywhere: at the swimming pool, in the park, at the cinema, just like Francis does, just like all of us in the staff room do. He overreacted to an instinct that follows him everywhere – for the safety of his daughters. I recall my many phone calls to the local council complaining about the high hedges around the play park near our house because paedophiles can hide in them. They clearly think I'm nuts. The hedges look lovely, and everyone likes them. It's only me that imagines them as great hiding spots for adult men.

There are around 68,000 registered sex offenders living in the UK out of a population of 68 million. That's only 0.1 per cent of the population, so, in reality, they aren't everywhere. But when you spend so much of your working day with them, you become ultra vigilant. Even an innocent man learning to swim looks like a pervert.

***

It's my final meeting with Lenny before his Parole Board in a month. It's an opportunity for final assessments before making a recommendation either for his release on licence or for him to remain inside. He's a disarmingly handsome man with penetrating green eyes. In his thirties, he has olive skin and a shock of thick, long dark brown hair, which is tied in a bun. With his leather bracelets and rope necklaces, one with a crucifix pendant, he looks like he's headed to a music festival. Someone who's all about peace and love, man. I normally find this look endearing, but not on Lenny.

We've spoken about his history on previous occasions, and we talk again about his experiences growing up in a loving and supportive family. He describes a comfortable upbringing. Well-educated, from a nice neighbourhood. He says he had everything any child could desire in life and subsequently tried to replicate the 'perfect' relationship he saw between his parents with his own wife. His partner continues to support him even after his offences and now in prison. He was employed as a youth worker and claims that he trained for the role, so that he could share some of his 'life's blessings' with young people who had not had the good fortunes enjoyed by him. I have contacted his old employers, who describe him as diligent and professional. 'A bit of a bighead, but nonetheless, popular with the teenagers, he did some good work with them. Everyone is shaken, we never saw this coming.'

Back in our interview, he's bragging about how many books he has devoured since we last met, then waits, presumably for me to be impressed and to compliment him on his achievements. He throws out long and unusual words that I'm unfamiliar with, and I feel inadequate. Conscious of shuffling in my seat as we face each other, I hold my hands under the desk. He has good eye contact, in contrast to most offenders, who look at their laps, but somehow, it's a little much. He stares defiantly at my face, like he's trying to get a read on me. I won't let him. He makes me uncomfortable. Trying to remain still and match his confidence, I tell myself that I'm professional, that nothing scares me and that I'm safe. On the other hand, I'm just a woman sitting in a small room alone with a man who rapes little girls.

It all began when Lenny's wife befriended their next-door neighbour who had a five-year-old daughter. The neighbour's husband regularly worked abroad, making it difficult for her to arrange childcare. Lenny offered to babysit. He was a charming youth worker, DBS checked, married to a lovely, gentle woman. Why wouldn't she trust him? They were friends after all and she was just thankful for the opportunity to go out, sometimes with Lenny's wife. Lenny babysat on several occasions before committing any crime, although in these matters it's hard to know for sure. You don't need the details, but what he did was enough for him to be locked up for ten years, though in my opinion this was far too lenient.

Together, we discuss his offences at length. Rather than try to explore why he did it, he claims 'I did it, so I can stop doing it.' He doesn't question why he did it, nor does he display the feelings of self-loathing so common in other sex offenders. He doesn't appear to be excited by the prospect of not offending anymore. In view of this, it is difficult to get a satisfying emotional response from him. He smiles with his mouth, but it doesn't reach his eyes. I have no doubt that, given the opportunity, he would do it again.

He hasn't described any events in his life that might explain his behaviour. He says the right things, that he is sorry, that he understands how he made the victim and her family feel, the long-term repercussions for her, but it all rings false. His remorse is unconvincing, like he's learned the language but not the meaning. He is arrogant, cocky and condescending, much more interested in his rights than his wrongs. He complains about the food and the conditions in prison, deflecting focus from his crimes. I can only conclude that he remains a dangerous criminal. I keep second-guessing myself though. I *really* don't like him and I fear it's clouding my professional judgement.

At the five-year point of his sentence, it's time to determine his suitability for parole. First, I check out his living arrangements, starting with a home visit to his wife. Her house is beautifully presented and she looks great, dressed in flattering clothes; she's just as attractive and charming as Lenny. I want to ascertain why she has stuck with him. It is surprisingly common for the partners of sex offenders to do so. She has moved to another area in readiness for his to return to her, as he won't be allowed near the victim's home, but she doesn't appear to mind the upheaval given her commitment to him. During our meeting she's adamant she wants him back and describes her excitement at the possibility of his release on parole.

'Do you regret that as Lenny will remain on the sex offender register even after his release, you'll never be allowed to have children and remain together?'

'I can't have children anyway,' she replies, defensively. 'We tried.'

I change the subject. 'What was it like living with him before he went to prison?'

'He always liked a tidy home and used to follow me around and check that I had done a good job of the housework. He liked me to read the same books as him, so that we could discuss them. It's been nice to read what I want to these past five years, so I'll have to get used to reading what he wants me to again if he gets out.'

'So, did you find him overbearing?'

'He was only doing it to help me. He liked the housework to be done "properly" and he chose our books so I could be better read. He wanted me to learn, be more intelligent.'

I'm desperately trying not to make assumptions about him.

'Could you describe a typical evening with him?'

'That's one thing that has been nice about him being away, I can watch what I want to on television. I was never able to when he was home.'

'Do you want him to come home? Are you excited by the prospect of his return?'

She hesitates before saying yes.

I'm not convinced. She hasn't mentioned any domestic abuse, but there are clear signs of coercive control. She just doesn't seem to have noticed or has otherwise persuaded herself that his total domination over her is alright. She has remained in contact with him throughout the five years that he has been in prison and maintains that she loves him. I can only judge how he made me feel: unnerved and self-conscious. Does he make her feel like that too? Does he still have power over her? She says their relationship is based upon mutual respect and she enjoys the 'support' he offers her, but I can't help having doubts.

The Parole Board will view a secure home life as being a protective factor against reoffending and could allow him to return to her. Her characterisation of him and the stability of their relationship will form part of the decision as to whether to release him. It's critical Lenny maintains his influence over her.

The day of the parole hearing has arrived. Parole Boards are an independent body who carry out assessments to ascertain if a prisoner is safe to be released from prison. They are usually chaired by a retired judge and involve the prisoner, their legal representative, an advocate representing the victim, psychiatrist, prison officer, inside Probation Officer and outside Probation Officer. The outside Probation Officer is me.

Having received the relevant documents before going to the prison, I see that it is going to be chaired by Judge Smith. I find all judges terrifying, their absolute confidence in their own decisions, their calm delivery, never an ounce of nerves or hesitation, but Judge Smith has the added dimension of being a notoriously difficult man, known for his dislike of Probation Officers. Respectfully known as the 'Silver Fox', now that hunting foxes is illegal, he's taken up Probation Officer baiting as his new favourite sport and I'm his latest target. While he is now an elderly man, he hasn't lost any of the dynamic gravitas of his younger years and relishes the opportunity to wield the power he enjoyed as a judge in court. As I leave the office, Mick helpfully tells me that Judge Smith is 'going to rip me a new arsehole' if I don't agree with him.

I have a white-knuckle drive to the prison, my palms clammy with anxiety. I find Parole Board hearings nerve-wracking at the best of times, but this one is going to be even worse. On a recent visit a gleeful prison officer told me how they love to stand outside Parole Board meetings and listen in. They particularly enjoy it when Judge Smith is chair, the entertainment of listening to him shouting at poor, hapless Probation Officers too good a 'comedy show' to miss.

Lenny has an exemplary prison record. A model prisoner, he has completed all the sex offender programmes and complied with everything asked of him. Prison staff have been impressed with his willingness to engage and have found him to be an enthusiastic member of all discussion groups. He is helpful, has stayed out of trouble and the reports provided by the prison suggest that he is ready to be released, a view Judge Smith has already indicated he supports. As the prison officer reads out his report, Judge Smith nods along encouragingly. The entirely male parole panel provide unanimously glowing accounts of how well Lenny has done. Judge Smith looks over to Lenny and smiles, clearly vicariously proud that the criminal justice system has succeeded in its stated ambition to rehabilitate this well-read, well-spoken man from a good background who had a momentary lapse of judgement. Then it's my turn. All eyes are on me. I feel sick at what I'm about to say. The audacity to disagree with all of them.

    I open with my credentials, my years of experience of working with sex offenders, emphasising that I understand their extensive range of manipulation techniques, how many sex offenders are skilled at 'playing the game'. Yes, he's been well behaved, yes, he's said all the right things and done all the right things, but I think he's lying. I have a 'feeling', a hunch. I'm conscious it's not actual evidence, but given my experience, I'd like to describe it as professional judgement. Quite rightly, this isn't enough, and I need to say why. I desperately want to plead from the heart: he's dangerous, he gives me the creeps. I've questioned my reasoning for wanting to turn down his parole application over and over again, and I know that it's more than just not liking him. He's talked about how much he has learned from the sex offender programme and his positive plans for release, including the support of his wife, the new address, the possibility of a job, and though his wife didn't look too excited about it, she categorically said she wants him back. I still have a nagging feeling. I can't say those things in a professional meeting, so instead, I close limply and state yet again, 'In my professional judgement, he's not ready for release and should remain in custody.'

And Judge Smith goes off like a bag of fireworks. Shouting at me, in his incredibly posh, booming voice. Gesticulating accusatorily. The prison officers outside are bound to be glued to the door, laughing. He is toying with me, using words I don't understand. I feel hot and red, staring at him while he berates me and finding different ways of insinuating I'm stupid. He clearly captained the debate team at boarding school when he was four. With my poor comprehensive school education I am absolutely no match for him.

I want to cry but keep repeating that Lenny is a clever man. He knows exactly how to play the system and has done so very well during this sentence. I'm floundering; everyone else on the panel is looking at me with a mixture of pity and relief they'd voted 'right'. Lenny too is watching, his face smug. It's that smug look that has underpinned my feelings that he shouldn't be released, but I can't shout 'Look at his face! You're all wrong! He's a control freak – he checks his wife's housework! He tells her what to read and what to watch on telly!' I am perfectly aware this is a losing battle, but I just *know*. Despite the humiliation of what I'm going through now, I must be true to the assessment I've made, so I can't agree with them.

Finally, it is Lenny's turn to speak. He describes how the sex offender programme has helped him to change, he talks about the love and support of his family. He is so convincing even I start to believe him and wonder if I got it all wrong. He is getting sympathetic nods from the panel, who are taking it all in. Lenny is on a roll, looking triumphant, convinced that his parole is in the bag. And then, with peak confidence, he finishes his speech by describing how his five-year-old victim was dancing in front of him in a 'provocative' way – otherwise he wouldn't have done it.

And there it is. The façade has slipped. He has given himself away with that one word. I can see the faces of the members of the panel transform, twisting from impressed to disgusted in unison. I flash an 'I told you so look' at everyone in the room. Lenny's face is contorted with rage, further reflecting his real nature. He realises what he's done… The Board is adjourned. Ten minutes later we are asked to return, and Lenny's parole is refused. He can't apply for a further two years and must undertake another sex offender treatment programme. I want to punch the air and shout: 'See, I knew, I told you!', but instead the face I've learned to control remains impassive.

Judge Smith doesn't say thank you to anyone and as he leaves, looks at me with a disgruntled expression. I'm most pleased. Lenny remains safely locked up and my original arsehole is intact.

I recognise that I've got lucky on this occasion. There is much to be said about the gut feeling, but everyone else in that room had their gut feelings too and we were all convinced we were right. I think again about the importance of experience, of being able to draw upon knowledge you've already learned from other offenders, of listening, not missing a single word, having regular visits and really getting to know someone. Too often Probation Officers' jobs are consumed by form filling and box ticking, which provide scant insight into the essence of a person. My first suspicions about him came when he said, 'I did it, but I can stop if I want to' rather than 'I did it, but I don't know how to stop.' His entitlement, his need for control, were embedded in his language from the start.

My sense of vindication is short-lived though, when I consider that I'll have to see him again. It is a big decision to deny someone their liberty, made even more difficult by the ongoing relationship after the fact. I doubt Lenny trusted me before. He certainly won't now, and I'm sure he will be mindful of every single word he says to me henceforth, making the job of assessing him even more opaque.

Denying a parole application in front of an inmate can be dangerous for Probation Officers. This was illustrated to me a few years back when an inmate whispered in my ear, 'I'll kill you when I get out.'

(I think he forgot.)

***

The question of whether to grant parole remains incredibly difficult. Today, there is a debate raging in the staff room. My colleagues Hannah and Chris have jointly visited a dangerous sex offender, called Edward, currently in prison. He is well into his seventies, frail and in very poor health. He has been a regular and serious offender since the mid-1960s. He's committed a range of sexually motivated offences including kidnap, torture and rape. The discussion is about whether he should be released from prison on licence. He hasn't committed any offences lately, despite having been out on licence for several months recently. He was recalled to custody after admitting that he still had a fondness for young girls and it was felt that he therefore still posed a risk. Not so different a character to Colin Pitchfork, who murdered two young girls in the 1980s and whose eventual parole and recall in 2021 prompted public outcry, we know that Edward is a high-profile case and any decisions made about him will be open to scrutiny and danger.

Hannah believes his risk is currently higher because he has 'nothing to lose' by committing one last offence in view of his declining health. The prison Probation Officer, however, feels that the fact he didn't actually commit any offences last time he was out – only fantasised about it – coupled with his age and frailty, indicates he no longer poses any risk and should therefore be released. In any event, he will be released in six months when his sentence ends. But the question is: does the public need another six months of protection from him, or can he be released on licence with extra oversight and some degree of knowledge gathered about his behaviour from within the community? In either case, given his comprehensive history, he would be monitored according to the sex offender register, where the police can do spot checks and insist on conditions such as him not living near his victims. But if he is released at the end of his sentence, there would be no *additional* monitoring. If he is released on licence he would be monitored for the entire six-month period that he would still have been in prison, with tags and curfew. His case has been fully discussed at MAPPA (Multi-Agency Public Protection Arrangements) and several agencies are involved, most notably the mental health team and social services, with the police and probation playing the central roles.

To fully evaluate this problem, in their interview with Edward, Hannah and Chris asked a host of probing inquiries.

We must ask shockingly intimate questions of all sex offenders, and this interview was no exception. Chris remarks that he sat in silence for most of it watching Edward's face. Witnessing this type of consultation feels very different to conducting it yourself and, though we all conduct similar interviews every day, Chris admitted it was unsettling remaining passive. Unusually for the Probation Service, Hannah has a similar background to some of the barristers in the Crown Court, having been educated at a private boarding school; like them, she has an amazing ability to 'throw' her voice. In these moments she has such an air of confidence, expertise and authority, you can almost see the recipient quake. Chris said that, despite Edward's history, he too looked perturbed by Hannah's questioning. She is perfectly aware of her strengths and uses them to great effect.

The interview went something like this:

> Hannah: Do you still masturbate?*
> Edward: I can't get an erection anymore.
> Hannah: Do you still get aroused?
> Edward: Yes.
> Hannah: What do you do with it then.

---

* This is a question we all ask our clients a lot, it doesn't even feel weird or embarrassing anymore. I have used this example of somebody else asking about masturbation as one day my mum will read this and I don't want her to know that I spend my days asking old blokes what they toss off about. It is, in fact, how I spend quite a bit of my time. A soul-destroying and miserable task... but strangely satisfying when one of them says they now toss off about something appropriate.

Edward: I hold on to it even though it's soft.
Hannah: What do you think about when you're holding it?
Edward: All the girls I've abused in the past.

The interview continued in this vein with Hannah probing and asking questions about his sexual fantasies. The upshot of the interview being that he still thinks about offending but lacks the physical capacity to enact his fantasies.

Mick helpfully pipes up with 'Oh! The memory bank wank!' The sombreness of the conversation is immediately diffused by his reliably inappropriate humour, and we all laugh.

The consensus agreed, both at MAPPA and in the staff room, is that he should be given parole. I recognise this may be upsetting, especially for his victims, however, it also allows for six months of information gathering about his daily routines. All the information will be shared with the police and any other relevant agency, so it will help them to continue to monitor him during the term of his licence, then afterwards, on a less rigorous basis, as part of his sex offender registration. He will only be out six months earlier, but if left to complete his entire sentence he would be released without this extra and largely free to do what he wants. It's very difficult to know what to do with dangerous offenders at the tail end of their lives. Mick remarks that keeping them in prison till they die doesn't sound half bad. In the event, Edward was released on licence and, even if he may have wanted to commit further offences, his body prevented him from hurting anyone. He only lived for six months after his release. No tears were shed for him when he died.

***

Since 2022 the Parole Board has stopped accepting recommendations from Probation Officers and prison staff. From a selfish perspective, there are some merits in this, one of them being that inmates who have their parole turned down won't want to kill their Probation Officer anymore. Besides, it's easier for criminals to connect with people they know can't determine when or if they leave prison. However, the reforms completely undermine the expertise and experience that probation and prison officers have, and the new regime was brought in, unsurprisingly, without consultation. So instead of decisions being made by people who can assess the offender by regularly interviewing them and getting to know them, those decisions about parole are made by people who rely only on reports that cannot capture the nuances of human behaviour.

In Lenny's case, he would certainly have been released because he ticked all the boxes. I fully believe that considering his feelings of entitlement, his conviction, his lust for power, sex and control he would have abused again quickly. His belief that he had beaten the system would have increased his risk. But what do I know?

13

Petra

It's MAPPA (Multi-Agency Public Protection Arrangements) meeting day! This is a monthly meeting with other agencies, including the police, social services, mental health and housing, to discuss the most dangerous offenders on our caseloads. As Probation Officers typically have the most interaction with offenders, we act as project manager in each case. We share information about progress and risk with the mental health team, while the police provide updates on any intelligence, housing or neighbourhood issues, and social services on children. We can assign each other tasks, like requesting phone and computer checks by police, or specific medication or courses with the offender's mental health team or additional appointments with probation.

I love the chance to discuss clients with other agencies. At a time when inquiries into serious further offences, such as some recent high-profile paedophile rings, always cite the lack of information sharing, MAPPA is a fine example of how effective inter-agency work is at reducing risk.

These meetings also provide an opportunity to moan about how busy we all are and draw red exclusion lines on maps so that perpetrators can't go near to their victims. (We usually add a few extra miles, for good measure.)

Thankfully, my MAPPA meeting went off without incident and I'm getting ready to see my client Petra when Mick comes running into the office fresh from his meeting. He's been discussing Glen.

Glen is a thirty-five-year-old father of two and a plumber who downloads indecent images of children. He was released from prison on licence twelve months ago. In view of his record, he has been assessed as high risk and must be seen by Mick weekly. This kind of intensive intervention is hard, draining work, especially with Glen, who – disowned by his family and with no prospect of ever working in people's houses again given there could be children present – likes nothing better than to moan and feel sorry for himself. He regularly discusses how he'd like to end it all but he manages to come back each week. They have spent the last year addressing Glen's behaviour, talking about how there *are* victims out there, even though Glen hasn't personally touched them, and developing systems to avoid future offending, such as avoiding the dark web and not paying to look at underage porn.

Lately, it appeared that Glen had 'got it'. He was no longer feeling so sorry for himself and seemed to grasp the monumental hurt he has caused by looking at real children, who really exist, and who have been abused in the making of images he sought out for his own enjoyment. At his previous MAPPA meeting, police reported that there was nothing suspicious on his phone or laptop, and Mick learned there had been some positive contact with his ex-wife. Mick had been dancing around the office before today's meeting – finally, he could downgrade Glen to medium risk and meet with him every fortnight, instead of seeing the 'self-absorbed tosser every bloody week. I'll be glad to see the back of him.'

But his excitement was short-lived. A neighbourhood constable had been invited to the meeting to share his knowledge about Glen. The officer had spotted Glen in a local park standing in a circle with several other men around a prostrate woman stretched out on the grass. The police officer apprehended them and ascertained that the woman was a 'Greek Goo Girl'. Everyone around the table goes quiet – nobody knows what on earth a 'Greek Goo Girl' is. The Greek bit turned out to be a red herring – she just happened to be from Greece. They were all masturbating on her, hence the 'Goo'. Apparently, being a 'Goo Girl' is a growing trend amongst sex workers who have discovered they can make money while lying still. This indignity is preferable to having sex – much less effort involved. Tossing off over a woman with a group of men isn't reassuring behaviour, so Glen's high-risk status remains, and the weekly visits are reinstated. Mick remarks that it's an improvement as at least it involves consenting adults now and this specific act presents a brand-new avenue for discussion.

What nobody wants to admit is that, even within prisons, it's hard to know what inmates are up to. Outside, no matter how many sessions offenders attend, how closely they're monitored by however many agencies, we simply can't know everything. Sadly – and alarmingly – the police have a reputation for keeping vital information to themselves. This is especially evident in domestic abuse situations where there have been numerous call-outs, but no prosecution. Thus, evidence of an offender's history of abuse is often completely unknown to the Probation Officers supervising them. I've found that building friendships and connections within the police is the most effective way to gain information, but this really shouldn't be the case. It is deeply concerning that opportunities to improve public safety are frequently missed through failures in information sharing between agencies, which tend not to have a legal obligation to do so. Today, however, the police very quickly shared the new intelligence, which has proved to be an opportunity for Mick to appear incompetent. Ignorant as he was about Glen's new 'hobby', he is embarrassed because the police knew about the 'goo' before he did.

My thoughts drift back to Petra. She isn't the usual kind of probation client; she looks like she's straight out of a film, a sophisticated, polished woman. Always clad in a chic, well-fitting business suit, flaunting manicured hands and tastefully dyed blonde hair tied in an artful 'messy' bun, she strikes just the right combination of casual and smart – like she hasn't tried too much. She is sixty-eight, but her complexion is bright and youthful. Certain she must have had a face lift, I look for the tell-tale scars around her ears but they are invisible, artfully covered up by tendrils of hair – or simply non-existent! She makes me feel scruffy in the shabby little interview room we are in, even though I've made a special effort today, as I do every week for her appointments. It's obvious to all my colleagues – Mick looked me up and down this morning, saw my carefully made-up face and best court suit and chirped: 'Seeing Petra today then?'

PETRA

Petra is an interior designer and stylist. She promotes her company to wealthy international clients, travelling business class to design and furnish their plush and opulent homes and offices. I fight the urge to bring some Dulux colour cards and photos of my kitchen for some free advice.

She was released from prison six months ago. She had been inside for just over a year. It wasn't her first time, but she views it as a break, a time to 'collect her thoughts', maybe change her name again, have a rest from running her business. She tells me that she finds prison refreshing, a view so unusual to everyone else in there it's as though she occupies a different universe. She oozes charm and social ease. She's the type of person whose air of entitlement is so ingrained it's infectious. Prison officers have admitted, with no sense of irony, that during her incarceration, she was known as the 'Princess' and treated accordingly. She managed to obtain extra privileges, such as more time in the exercise yard. Both staff and inmates trailed her, serving her meals and cleaning her cell. And clearly, I'm not immune either, stood here in my Sunday best.

Petra has fraudulently accrued millions of pounds from her various businesses and would rather like some more. As she sits across the desk from me, I can't help but wonder if I admire or despise her. Petra is greedy. A con woman, a fraudster. She's been doing it for decades. It's her life, she thrives on the excitement of it all. She has planned and designed interiors everywhere from Dubai to Shanghai, but never provided the goods that the customers paid for, before changing her name, deleting her website, erasing all evidence that her business existed, then moving on and inventing some new way to extort money.

The police are convinced that she has committed substantially more offences than she has been caught for, but finding out what she has done has proved difficult, because many victims don't wish to press charges. Embarrassed at being fooled into paying out large amounts of money by a woman, they prefer to write the losses off.

'I'm never doing it again,' she huffs dramatically. 'I'm too old for prison, it reminds me of boarding school. It used to be all right, but I need my home comforts now. I'm going straight. This time my business will be legitimate.'

I'm not convinced. She has already breached the terms of her licence as her conditions clearly state that she's not allowed to own another business. She happily tells me about her new venture, and I remind her again that she's not supposed to have one and that I can recall her to prison.

'You won't though, will you sweetie?'

Petra is so confident of getting her own way that, while I am irritated by her condescending tone, I feel a shiver of excitement, sure that she won't be getting the upper hand this time.

***

It unravelled when I called the police to ask if they had any information about Petra and her current business as I *was* planning to recall her to prison. It was then that I was introduced to Tony, a detective who had been involved in her last arrest and had been researching her crimes for years. He was aware of the new venture, but as it all appeared to be legitimate, he started questioning me about what I knew.

I've asked many Probation Officers around the country if they have ever joined forces with the police on any cases outside of MAPPA and it is highly unusual – in my own experience I've only done it once before and, though there are currently moves to promote more inter-agency working, it isn't standard practice to work together, despite us sharing the same clients. But this is an unusual case, and clearly the police think that probation might be useful, so I have agreed to help them. Petra being seen every week is part of her licence conditions, so I have plenty of opportunity to investigate and have confirmed with Tony that I won't recall her until we have gained further information on her current activities.

I'm in an exclusive, well-heeled village outside of town, parked beside electric gates which slowly open to allow me in. As I proceed up the long gravel driveway in my clapped-out old car, it is difficult not to conclude that crime does pay if you're clever, and wonder if the odd spell in prison might well be worth it. Petra is waiting for me on the steps of her grand house, looking chic as ever. As usual, I feel insecure.

'So, you've come to see my little company! I can't wait to show you.'

Having already browsed her beautifully presented website, selling carefully curated homeware and household goods at affordable prices that 'anyone can have', I am intrigued to see what she has in stock – mainly so I can pinch some ideas for my house. The hundreds of positive reviews suggest that the items she is selling really are as luxurious as they look in the pictures and I've been wondering if she is perhaps 'going straight' after all.

Petra invites me to join her in a golf cart as we motor across a manicured lawn to a track. I consider how Tom would love a garden big enough to go jogging in – he loves jogging and therefore his lung capacity is enormous. Staring out as we drive along, I think back to this morning which began as most do. He is a morning person, all jolly and talkative while I'm desperately trying to carve out a little more sleep. Tom tries to wake me by whispering that he loves me in my ear, which tickles, but I still ignore him. He then starts telling me I'm wonderful, then flicks my jowls and pokes at my wrinkles. Then he gets bored and starts yawning, his mouth still near my ears. He sucks in lungs-full of air. I feel like he's sucking the very life out of me via my ear. He snorts back into it again and gets up, putting the radio on very loudly on his way out of the room. I rub my ears, and the side of my face is wet. Tom has either dribbled or snotted on me. He looks happy, dancing around the bedroom to his morning disco. I have no choice but to get up and go to work.

I'm still thinking of him and admiring Petra, who is single and doesn't have to contend with these morning rituals, when we arrive at a huge, converted barn. Inside, it is full of stuff, much like an Amazon warehouse. She obviously has stock. She sees the expression of surprise on my face and is pleased.

'I'm going to be Britain's answer to Jeff Bezos – but better looking!' she laughs.

There are a couple of women sorting out goods and wrapping them into neat parcels and in a small office another woman is working at a desk.

'Susan, meet Liz, my Probation Officer. Liz, this is Susan, my secretary.'

Petra introduces us without a shred of embarrassment about who I am. She appears to view me as one of her minions and I am suddenly waved aside as she wanders off into the warehouse, leaving Susan and me alone. The moment she is out of earshot, Susan begins, cautiously.

'I'm so pleased you're here. Petra is at it again. She's been trying to pay me in *jewellery*. I haven't received a proper pay cheque in weeks, nor have the other staff! I've got a pile of complaints from people who haven't received their goods. I can't believe I've fallen for it again. Petra insisted it was legitimate this time, but it's just bullshit.'

As Petra comes back, I quickly scribble my number down and hand it to Susan.

'Call me.'

For the next few weeks, Susan calls me daily, providing me with the full details of Petra's income and outgoings – which is nearly all income. Susan relishes having a good root through the paperwork and passing on information.

'Why didn't you tell the police?' I enquire during one phone call.

'I was so embarrassed I fell for it again. I've worked for her before and the same thing happened, but she seemed different this time. She's so convincing when she says that she's changed. I believed her. Plus, I was worried that I might be implicated and could get into trouble, so it feels safer talking to you.'

Without my consent, Susan also provides the angry customers Petra has currently swindled with my phone number; they are desperate for answers and keen to talk to someone. Many hadn't considered calling the police as the website looked legitimate, there had been many positive reviews, and they genuinely believed items had been lost in the post. In contrast to her former businesses, which relied on ripping off hugely wealthy companies, this time she is defrauding ordinary people; young couples furnishing their first houses, people who had saved up to create rooms that look as beautiful as those on Petra's lavish website. The people on the phone were devastated, having lost their savings on what they expected to be beautiful items of furniture and household goods. I become their first port of call before I pass them on to Tony at the police station. Petra is becoming a full-time job, and I find myself struggling to accommodate this investigation among my other fifty-five clients.

Following weeks of listening to victims and Susan, who still hasn't been paid, any shred of admiration I had for Petra has evaporated. We now have enough information for her to be arrested on new charges and she has freely admitted that she has started a new business, which contravenes the terms of her licence. It's time for her to be recalled to prison and it is with a sense of relief that I can get rid of all the extra work she has created. Tony and I arrange for him to come and arrest her. We are both busy and with some difficulty arrange a mutually suitable time for Petra's next appointment, which I have squeezed in between two other people, so I hope her arrest will be quick.

After calling her into the office and exchanging platitudes, a feeling of guilt sweeps over me. I don't like being underhand and while Petra may be con artist who has taken large amounts of money from innocent people, when she's sitting in front of me, I just don't feel right about it. I'm supposed to protect the public by rehabilitating people. I'm not a police officer. Undetected by Petra, Tony has followed her in and arrests her for breaching her licence and for committing further offences. Petra has an expression of pure surprise. She never once suspected that I would carry out my duty and call the police. I explain to her that I had no choice.

'It's okay, Liz. Honestly, you're just doing your job. I completely understand. I've been very foolish.'

Her graciousness makes me feel even more wretched. Despite her glossy exterior, she suddenly looks smaller, diminished. I'd like to hug her, but instead Tony puts her in handcuffs, and I accompany them down the steep back stairs. Tony walks down backwards keeping Petra steady while I walk behind them. Suddenly Petra stumbles, groans and holds on to her chest. Shocked, Tony loses his footing and falls backwards. Tied together with the handcuffs, they both tumble down the stairs, Petra, unmoving, landing on top of Tony. I take her pulse; she's alive. I wipe the hair from her face to look at her eyes and can't resist peaking for signs of the facelift. I spot the scar and immediately feel ashamed. We manage to unlock the cuffs and disentangle a trapped Tony before calling for an ambulance urgently, asking them to be quick, Tony muttering 'Fucking hell, this is all I need,' while rubbing his back. I can see he's hurt, but he won't admit it.

I'm also worrying about being behind with a waiting room full of angry criminals as it's getting late and nod my agreement to Tony; it's all I need too. While we wait for the ambulance, we discuss how busy we both are, then start to laugh about sitting on the stairs with an unconscious woman, who, incidentally, still looks more put together than either of us.

Tony goes off in the ambulance with Petra and I call Susan to let her know.

'It's karma. She deserves it.'

I realise I don't feel that bad for Petra either.

Later, a call from Tony. He confirms her heart attack was fatal.

***

Tony and I go the funeral to make sure she's dead and inadvertently double the congregation. It hadn't occurred to me that Petra wouldn't be popular; materially she had it all. In contrast to what Petra had described as a happy childhood, she was sent to boarding school in England while her parents enjoyed a frivolous and bohemian life abroad. They rarely returned home and Petra was left with various nannies, none of whom she formed a bond with. Petra was lonely and miserable – she didn't know how to have relationships, let alone sustain them, and continued to be alone her entire life.

I realise that she never experienced the intimacy of private jokes and secret laughter. I think of conversations Tom and I have that keep us grounded. Only this morning Tom observed that it's a shame my arse is disappearing and turning into an old lady bottom. I say that he too is losing his bottom at the same time as developing his stomach and those on top of his thin legs makes him look like a pantomime chicken. He says that now my bottom has almost entirely disappeared

I look like a heron. We chortled in the sound knowledge that we love each other. Nobody has been around to make Petra laugh. Accumulating wealth has been Petra's way of filling the void left by her absent family.

Despite her very different, highly privileged background, it is an inescapable truth that Petra was never properly loved. It is an experience she shares with so many of the criminals I see. I wonder if love really is the key to not offending.

Tony continues to investigate Petra and ensure that the proceeds of her crimes are recouped.

At home later, I wonder what has happened to me. I joined the Probation Service because I like people and want to help to facilitate better lives. I am now so overworked and stressed that I seem to have lost any capacity to care about any one of them. All compassion has gone. I was genuinely angry with Petra for having a heart attack and putting me behind on my work. I can honestly say that I got some pleasure from stamping her file 'Deceased'. One less client.

I don't like myself anymore: I've become numb, and constantly stressed.

***

I may as well take this opportunity to tell you about the one other case I worked on with the police. It was before MAPPA was introduced in 2001 as part of the Criminal Justice and Court Services Act 2000. It was in the days when agencies scarcely spoke to each other unless they really had to; well, apart from the odd occasion when my line manager went to the pub with his mate in the CID and he would come to work the next day with some notes about various offenders literally written on the back of a packet of fags.

This was before I met Tom. I was a single parent living alone with my eighteen-month-old daughter. On the news there is a horrifying story of a young girl being murdered on the other side of the country. No culprit has been found. Police up and down the country are required to re-examine all the paedophiles on their records to look for suspects. I am supervising a paedophile on licence who has spent many years in prison following a record of kidnapping and abusing children. He is one of around a hundred paedophiles who fit the possible modus operandi of the murderer. My line manager and his mate from the CID discuss him at their monthly outing to the pub and cook up a plan for me to obtain information by 'befriending' him.

Let's call him Trevor.

Trevor is clearly a psychopath, displaying many of the classic traits: a grandiose opinion of himself, lack of guilt, lack of empathy, superficially charming and, significantly for my line manager and his CID friend, he is not risk averse. I can pose as a friend, telling him that I only became a Probation Officer to gain contacts which would satisfy my own desires. So keen is Trevor to brag about his activities that he readily accepts this backstory and talks openly about what he is up to. I work closely with the police, passing on any information he divulges.

Trevor reveals he has a 'burner' phone and randomly calls numbers until he gets an answer from a child's voice. He then engages that child in conversation. Most soon hang up, but he calls so many numbers that he finds a small number of children who allow him to carry on calling them. He eventually befriends them, and once he gains their trust, he chooses a particular place to meet. During our conversations he shows me the telephone number and messages they've exchanged, which are friendly and immature, Trevor presenting as a fellow young person. I memorise the number while he's still talking – I can't hear what he's saying I'm so busy repeating the number in my head.

Trevor arranges to meet the child in the town where they live many miles away, and gives me details of where and when he is going. He excitedly tells me about a van he has secretly purchased and customised especially for the trip, and offers to show it to me since I am now his 'friend'. We agree that, for his next appointment, I'll meet him at his van. I tell the police where it is located and, though I'm relatively sure he genuinely trusts me, I'm not certain that it isn't a trap. As any woman knows, nothing good happens in a van. Given assurances by the police that I'll be safe as they will get there before me and park across the road in an unmarked car, my fears are somewhat alleviated.

On the outside his van looks incongruous, like any work van, but, shockingly, inside it is covered with pink fur. There are teddy bears and dolls, fur handcuffs and a mattress. There is nobody else around. No parked car, no plain-clothes police. I am alone with him. Terrified, horrified and disgusted. He invites me to get in. Making excuses about how I don't want to spoil his beautiful van, I tell him it's impressive enough for me to see from the outside, before heading back to my car. I try not to run, to look nonchalant, to have an expression that displays pleasure instead of horror. He looks surprised that

I'm not staying. Apologising profusely, I explain that I don't want my colleagues to suspect our friendship.

Immediately calling the police upon my return to the office, I'm told they forgot to go, but they are excited by the information. Furious, hurt and disappointed by their lack of care, I sit at my desk and sob.

The day Trevor planned to visit the child comes and the police are lying in wait for him. As the child approaches the van Trevor is arrested before any further harm can be done. This work has taken months. Gaining his trust, pretending to be his friend, remembering phone numbers. I dream about the phone numbers every night. I fear Trevor so much that, after months of living with the curtains closed, we move house.

The investigating police officers received commendations for their work. I never heard from them again. My line manager told me I'm the bravest person he's ever met and gave me a creme egg. He stops meeting the man from the CID for pints.

Trevor was sentenced to decades in prison and I never thought about him again, until one day many years later, the memory of him came to bite me on my flat arse.

14

Liz

It's Christmas Eve. I've been too busy at work to organise anything so not a single preparation has been made at home. There is a house full of visitors arriving tomorrow, all expecting a Christmas feast, and the fridge is *empty*. There are no ticks to confirm I've bought anything on our children's carefully written wish list of presents. 'I'm so excited for Christmas! You've been amazing at keeping it a secret this year. I have no idea what surprises you have in store!' my daughter Sophie exclaims happily. Smiling at her, there is the excruciating knot of panic behind my ribs. I also have no idea what surprises are in store beside the total lack of food or gifts.

I'm going to have to be quick if I'm to pull Christmas off. Nobody can know that I haven't done anything yet. At home, I find myself increasingly trying to cover my tracks, hiding the fact that everything is in turmoil, all while putting on what I hope comes across as a jovial air of confidence.

Christmas Eve: I glance at my messy desk, turn off my computer and pray I haven't made any cock ups. I dash out, offering hasty goodbyes. Now, I'm racing through the shopping centre, surrounded by blokes with the same worried expression. Even though it's last minute, I'm determined to catch up and make tomorrow a good day – thinking about the gifts I can buy for my family, hoping I'll find something special. But then, a wave of guilt hits me. I realise it's not just Christmas. I've been a terrible mother lately – too tired to connect with my family after work, too exhausted to cook anything nice and just not much fun to be around. This is my chance to make it right.

In the middle of the shopping centre, I spot Santa with an elf and pause, smiling to myself. There is a queue of children waiting and Santa has two on his lap. I give them another quick glance before heading up the escalator. It's odd – Santa looks *familiar*. In fact, so does the elf next to him. Coming down the adjacent escalator I see Rob, a police officer from the child protection unit. He smiles and says hello before he too turns to Santa and his elf, and then as we cross on the escalators, we both have the same slow-motion epiphany and whip back round.

Santa is one of our registered sex offenders. He is no longer on licence, but certainly *not* allowed to work with children. The elf next to him is his wife. Let's call them Jeffrey and Ghislaine. Ghislaine has significant learning difficulties. Even though she is in her late thirties, she looks about twelve. She is the perfect foil for Jeffrey, helping him to lure children. Ghislaine is actually quite lovely and I feel sorry for her. A sweet and innocent woman, she has the mental age of a seven-year-old and is of course a victim of Jeffrey herself. She doesn't understand what she has been doing. She really enjoys sex and firmly believes that allowing her to have sex with his network of friends has been a kindness bestowed upon her by

Jeffrey. The sad reality is that she has been used by a paedophile ring, both for sex and as a means to entice children. Her sweet disposition makes it easy for her to befriend children, who in turn become victims of Jeffrey's ring of friends.

Given her limited capacity to understand the consequences of her actions, she genuinely believes the children she gets for Jeffrey and his friends are happy about it. She is also a victim of sexual abuse. In a way it feels like a miscarriage of justice that she was also charged with sexual assault and sent to prison. She is now on the sex offender register with Jeffrey. If she'd been the actual socialite Ghislaine Maxwell, some of her relatives would have been invited on to the BBC to say how lovely she is, but as she is vulnerable and comes from a council house, nobody has stuck up for her apart from probation, who have referred her for counselling and sex education. Both have conditions not to see each other as part of their licence, so not only should they not be working with children now, but they also shouldn't be doing it together.

Hurrying back down the escalator, I find Rob waiting at the bottom. We agree it's best not to cause a scene or alarm the parents and children in the queue, so we quietly approach a security guard, explain the situation, and Rob calls for police back-up. In the meantime, we make idle small talk in an attempt to entertain the waiting families, fielding curious questions from the children who want to know why Santa and his elf have been hauled off by a security guard – who, in a mild panic, has also begun searching for an emergency stand-in Santa.

Jeffrey and Ghislaine are taken to the police station and arrested for breaching their sex offender registration terms. No doubt, whoever hired them without a proper background check is being swiftly dismissed. The whole incident takes a while, and by the time it's over the shops are closing. I've completely forgotten about my own Christmas plans.

As compensation for interrupting my shopping, I'm allowed to take two Santa gifts home for Josh and Sophie. It's only when I walk through my front door that it hits me: I never bought a turkey, and the entire family is coming for Christmas dinner. The cheerful buzz I'd felt from spending the day with excited children evaporates instantly. Once again, work has taken precedence over my family.

When I break the news that Christmas might be shit this year, Josh sighs, 'Why can't we have a normal mum?' Later, as our relatives sit around the table, each having brought their own food, they watch me with quiet concern while Sophie and Josh unwrap their 'My First Colouring Book' sets. I feel physically sick; the feeling that is a constant these days.

A miserable Christmas break later, there are eighty-one emails waiting for me back at work. It's not dissimilar to any Monday morning – not a single 'Happy New Year' or 'Hope you had a nice holiday'. Only two emails are jokes, the rest are actual work. The answering machine is full of reports of domestic abuse incidents, rampant in this supposedly sacred period, one of them involving a client who is on life licence and now has to be recalled. Another is an intelligence report from prison which indicates that Adam has become a fundamentalist. He has been heard offering advice and support to another inmate due for release, who is plotting to put a bomb in a church as soon as they get out. I've got a drunk, aggressive man in the waiting room wanting to see me. I only work part-time, and I'm supposed to be finished by 2 p.m. I resist the urge to scream 'Why don't you all just fuck off, what do you expect me to do about it?!'

It's 2013 and Chris Grayling, Secretary of State for Justice, has recently introduced his prison benchmarking plan to privatise probation, where he intends to split probation in two, less dangerous clients going to private companies and the more serious cases staying with the Probation Service to cut costs. The result is hugely increased caseloads. All of probation is now suffering for his stupid plan.

My colleagues have come back with similar tales. Walking through the corridor, I'm greeted by the ashen faces of my friends and workmates. The increasing workloads and staff shortages are making it almost impossible to keep up. The laughter that used to permeate the office has completely disappeared. Five of the fourteen Probation Officers I work with are off sick with work-related stress. There is no time to talk to each other. I'm not the only one who has started to behave erratically.

The domestic violence recall is dealt with first, as keeping the victim safe is a priority. I email a reply to the prison thanking them for telling me about Adam. As he's in prison, he is bottom of the list of priorities. I have a hunch that he's purposefully trying to jeopardise any chance of release at his next parole hearing, given how much he fears coming out. He's been waging more dirty protests and asking me to visit, but while I wish I could go and talk to him to find out what's behind this new development, my caseload prohibits this: I simply cannot justify the time it would take. So I move on to the next email feeling ever more guilty, with a building sense of hopelessness.

Compared to other agencies in the criminal justice system, probation is easy to access, so we get lots of enquiries from people who can't get information elsewhere. One of the messages is from a very affable man called 'Dougie'. He's a worried dad, concerned about his son and wants to know the truth. He promises that his son really is a lovely lad, and Dougie simply can't believe he stabbed his own wife. His son has told him that he didn't, but Dougie wants reassurance. He's torn, unsure whether to believe that his daughter-in-law, who he was always fond of, could really have given herself a flesh wound by stabbing herself to get his son arrested like his son told him. Dougie wants to believe his son, but once we've talked and discussed the logistics of his daughter-in-law stabbing herself in the *back*, he reluctantly agrees that his son isn't the kind-hearted man he thought he was.

I try to get through the eighty-one emails as quickly, and therefore as haphazardly, as possible; I am terrified that because of the overwhelming amount of work and my own compromised standards, someone is going to get hurt.

After crawling through the emails, answering machine messages and seeing the drunk man in the waiting room, I breathe a sigh of relief. It's 6 p.m., only four hours after I should have finished! Another day when I haven't cooked the dinner I'd promised my family. My life has slipped out of control, and I have started grasping at any opportunity to claw it back. Dressing Tom has proved to be a quietly satisfying pastime. He always wears what I want him to. I have achieved this by placing what I'd like him to wear underneath my least favourite items when I'm putting his washing away. He assumes I'd put what I want him to wear on top, so takes the clothes beneath, thus always wearing what I intended. It has become a daily source of amusement, and I believe myself to be a clever and accomplished housewife.

Following an outburst where I declared I couldn't cope anymore, we finally get a cleaner. I am absolutely elated. Tom would never agree that he is sexist, but now he can have two women cleaning up after him. When I get home from work the following week, Vanessa, the new cleaner, has been. The house is pristine. I haven't even changed her name. I love her! I love her more than I love my own family. Nevertheless, while her cleaning skills are nearly as good as Steve the murderer's, she hasn't erased the feeling of dread which grows in my stomach every day. I thought a tidy house might sort me out. I'm guessing Steve thought the same thing.

Taking Max out every morning to get some fresh air offers a glimmer of respite – I chat with other dog owners while Max takes the opportunity to sniff some bottoms. There's been no supervision in over a year and no access to counselling. In their absence, I tell Max about all my work problems. He looks engrossed. Explaining to him all the horrible things people get up to makes me feel much better and inspires me to try an experiment with clients. I wonder if I could do an hour's session only saying 'mmm' in different tones of voice and looking interested. I mention it to my friends at work and we decide to set it as a challenge: could we do it for a whole day? We succeed with relative ease. One of my clients even describes it as one of the best sessions he's ever had, presumably because I didn't interrupt or challenge him, though I did find out a shocking number of his secrets purely by looking interested and saying 'mmm' in different ways. It went well with the other Probation Officers too. We decide to adopt the method more regularly for those days when we're too tired to come up with any good ideas.

The notion to just nod and say 'mmm' to clients for a day was born out of absolute exhaustion. I'm on to my second cold this month. I never used to get ill, but lately I seem to catch every bug going around, so increasingly I have days off. I feel too unwell to go to work today and spend the day in bed feeling guilt-ridden as my colleagues shoulder my workload between them. I end up in bed for a week.

Conscious that I need some air, I take Max out for a stroll and experiment with walking with my eyes shut. I wonder if I could get all the way home without opening my eyes, just be led by the dog. I'm mesmerised by the moving patterns swimming behind my eyelids. Max would never make a guide dog and has buggered off. I walk quite a way with my eyes shut, confident of making the whole journey, but end up bashing into a tree and arrive home scratched and covered in leaves. My family already think I'm potty, so I tell them the dog pulled me over. Until the tree, it had been a most enjoyable jaunt. But the week off has not stopped me behaving unusually, constantly drifting off into a dream world. I'm not sure why.

When it's time to go to work again, Tom provides encouragement with some positive reinforcement techniques to make me feel better. 'You look lovely today in that dress, much better than yesterday. That looked terrible.' He hasn't quite gotten the hang of it.

Tom is worried that I might use this book as a vehicle to be mean about him in public and so I just want to take a moment to tell you how helpful he has been while I was unwell. He emptied the bins and brought me perfect cups of tea without being asked. He at no time mentioned that he wanted his own favourite kind of 'positive reinforcement' as a reward for doing any of this. He also brought me hot water bottles and generally fussed over me. He did all of this because he is an altruistic, kind and clever man, who is also *really* good looking. He constantly tells me that everything will be all right, which, despite not feeling very helpful, shows he's trying hard. Tom is never in a mood and so it's well worth putting up with him being untidy.

Dragged back to work, I quickly feel odd. Having taken a week off, there are almost two hundred emails waiting for me on my return. My head is swimming and the emails materialise illegibly. Wondering if I've got high blood pressure and that's causing me to feel lightheaded, I decide to ignore the emails and pop into town and buy a blood pressure monitor but get distracted by shoes. Sure that shoes will make me feel better, I buy a pair. I already bought some last week, but they didn't seem to cure anything – maybe this pair will.

Now I have buyers' remorse. I'm queasy because of the amount of money I've spent. I'd hoped the shoes would get rid of the dread, but now it's just mixed with nausea. I try to persuade myself that shoe purchasing is okay because they were reduced and I 'needed' them. It's a kind of cognitive dissonance.

As Probation Officers we work through cognitive dissonance all the time, such as with sex offenders who *know* feeling up their grandson is wrong but try to persuade themselves that the grandson is benefiting from it because it is 'love'. I can't stop buying shoes. There is no room in the cupboard and I must hide them anyway. The guilt is worsened by the fact that I know exactly what I'm doing. No blood pressure monitor has been purchased, and I shouldn't have wasted time in town, as I should have been preparing for a MAPPA meeting about a paedophile who is about to be released from prison.

Several clients live close to the police station where the MAPPA meeting is held so, deciding to do some home visits afterwards, I collect their files to take with me, ensuring they're up to date and reviewing any recent developments I might have missed. Once everything is ready, I head to the meeting. Unable to leave the files in the car for security reasons, I pick them all up, but in my haste to get into the meeting, I drop the entire stack and papers scatter across the pavement. I quickly gather them up, but now they're in a complete mess. A wave of heat rises in my face, and my stomach tightens, but I push through and enter the meeting, somehow managing to just about hold it together.

The meeting goes well. I've enjoyed drawing an exclusion zone on a map in red where the said paedophile won't be allowed to go and made it a bigger area just to ensure he'll have to walk further to see his family, which pleases the others in the meeting. We all agree that we are quietly being bastards, and we all have a chuckle and then the meeting is over. It's been relatively light-hearted despite the subject matter, but still, I'm relieved to be done.

Once back in the car I suddenly feel overwhelmed with heat. Sweating, I open the window and wonder if I'm going through the menopause. I haven't started the engine yet. I know I've got the home visits, but the files are in total disarray. I'm consumed with panic. I can't remember who I've got to see or where they live. Shuffling through the papers to find their addresses doesn't help; the more I look, the more of a mess the files become and the more panic-stricken I feel. I have no idea where I am. My overriding desire is to go home, but I can't remember where I live or how to get there. Confused, I try to breathe slowly and deeply but only manage short gasps of air. Everything is out of control, even my breath. 'Oh my God! I can't even remember how to breathe.' The more I try to get a grip of myself, the more I panic.

One of the police officers from the meeting comes out and knocks on the car window to ask if I'm all right. I can see him and hear him, but his words sound garbled, like he's talking underwater. I can't understand a word, so I simply stare at him. I think my mouth is opening and closing like a guppy as I try to speak, but nothing comes out. As far as he can tell, I must just look like a middle-aged woman having a hot flush. Smiling at him, wishing he'd go away, I'm aware of feeling humiliated, but not sure why and don't know how to say anything. I give him the thumbs up, and he looks reassured before walking away.

The next thing I know I'm home, having got there on autopilot. I can't recall driving. As soon as I arrive, I start to cry with the relief of being there, before taking myself off to bed, where I remain for another week. My head is permanently 'swimming'. I'm convinced I'm going to die. In addition to the fear of death is the sense that I must have forgotten something at work or messed up on a job, and the unshakeable feeling that my family now hates me.

A doctor signs me off work for three months. I am the sixth Probation Officer in my office off sick. I feel that I've let everyone down. I'm one of the cheerful ones, the person who jollies other people along, and now I'm dumping yet more work on my already overstretched colleagues. At home, I've gone from functioning wife and mother to someone who can barely get out of bed.

I just cannot wake up – and when I do it's only to feel guilty about letting everyone down before falling sleep again. I just can't get enough sleep. It's where I escape. My dreams are consumed with ways to remain asleep forever – I'm lying on the road about to be run over or sinking under the water in the river. The dreams are comforting, they make sense; when I'm awake I feel discombobulated. I can't concentrate, I walk into things, I forget my sentences halfway through. I'm scared. I believe that I've completely lost my mind; I don't recognise myself at all. The visit to the doctor confirmed that I have a stress-related illness (formally known as a nervous breakdown) and that the breakdown event happened after the MAPPA meeting, when my body said 'That's it, no more. I'm forcing you to rest.' My doctor tells me almost glibly that the condition is one of the hazards of working in any kind of social work. I realise that I've spent years in a state of panic because I don't have enough time to see everyone and do a good job and then at home try to be a half-decent wife and mother, while panicking about what I might have forgotten at work. My body has been in a permanent state of 'flight', infused with adrenaline. I'm exhausted. I'm encouraged to rest and take happy pills. I've never been out of control before. I don't like it.

After a fortnight spent entirely in bed I get up and wander around the house. Every sink is full of bristles and toothpaste, which is also splattered across the floor, there are skidders down the toilet, the dog hasn't had a proper walk in days and there is a ton of washing to be done. I need to pull myself together. My family is clearly incapable of looking after themselves. I may have gone a bit mad, but I can see that somebody's got to look after them and that somebody must be me.

Max the dog is the only one who understands. Josh and Sophie look at me with disappointment. I've become a terrible parent. I know they're young adults, but I need to pull myself together. Deciding to take them to a drive-thru, I hope this will start to make amends. They're very excited as finally we're doing something together again. I feel just about capable of driving and there is much happy chatter between Josh and Sophie in the car on the way. They give me a long list of what food they want. Arriving at the counter, and unable to remember a single thing they ordered, I simply 'drive through', giving the assistant a wave, which they return with a perplexed look. The angry faces of my children meet me in the rear-view mirror. We go to my parents' house for dinner instead, where my mother has adopted a permanent expression of worry and Sophie laments what an embarrassment I've become. She says that I constantly do 'crazy' things and that I'm completely unaware of it. As if to confirm this I give her a blank look, which is my calling card now. I am utterly helpless and unable to work anything out. The simplest of tasks is beyond me. At least I recognise my own ineptitude.

Back at home, Sophie has invited friends over. She looks happy again and, leaving them to it, I go and sit on the loo to have a think and pull myself together. Concluding that I haven't yet recovered, and I shouldn't have attempted to go out, I give myself permission to stay at home and rest for a bit longer.

I arise from my 'throne' and somehow manage to bash my nose on the toilet roll holder and it begins to bleed. There is no toilet roll left and, attempting to open a new one, I give myself a deep paper cut on my thumb, which also starts to bleed. I get up from the loo having wiped my face with my hand, covering it with more blood from my thumb. Blood is now spread across my face and up into my hair, which I now use to clean my hand. I have effectively blinded myself by wiping blood into my eyes. Standing in the bathroom I shout for help because I can't work out how to pull my tights up. Nobody comes, so, with pants and tights around my knees, I stumble and hop into the kitchen to get help only to find Sophie and her friends in there.

There is a stunned silence, followed by sniggering. My daughter's hands are over her face in horrified embarrassment. What has become of her professional, organised mother? I stand there in the kitchen with my bloody hair and face, mascara smeared up my forehead and pants around my knees. Despite the blindness I am not deaf and can hear their mockery. Apparently, as I leave there is further mirth as I have pulled my pants up over my dress. The next day I wake up with bruises on my face. I can't live like this. Soon the kids will be off to social services with their suitcases *pleading* to be re-housed. I know I should rest a bit more, but fear that if I carry on resting, I'll never get up. I need to do something about it.

Step One: Massage Course

I've always been interested in the connection between the lack of appropriate affection and the propensity for offending, having witnessed a recurring theme of neglect from the parents of the people I work with. Deciding that given my existing interest and the pressing need to settle my mind, I enrol on a short, taster massage course at a local spa while I'm off work. It is indeed relaxing and comes with the added bonus of getting treatments ourselves as we practise on each other. We are invited to join the spa team in their staff room, who all seem genuinely shocked by my perverse sense of humour, which I have dramatically toned down for their benefit. It is nothing like the staff room banter at the Probation Service. This new environment seems alien and bland. They discuss issues like what to have for dinner, and what colour to dye their hair, along with the constant dialogue about reality television programmes. I'm bored.

Objectively, probation is the more alien environment – laughing about burglars and court hearings in the staff room isn't exactly normal water-cooler conversation – but at least it's never boring.

At the end of the second day, we get some real customers to practise on: all elderly women, who have been widowed and are missing human touch and companionship. They are all on the plump side and massaging their soft flesh has the relaxing feeling of kneading dough. I can't help but have a watery, gloopy sound in my head to accompany the massage movements. The women talk of their families with love. While they have lost their husbands there is no talk of bitterness, crisis or chaos. They haven't used their loss as an excuse to commit a burglary or sexually assault their grandchildren. I am mystified by the strangeness of the unhealthy environment in which I've been working for the past twenty-five years. Most people lead quite simple, pleasant lives and seem kind and caring. I begin to wonder if the boredom and lack of excitement is a healthier way to live. I'd like to stay at home, have a laugh with my children and learn how to cook.

Step Two: See a Psychiatrist

Following three months off work, I return to see my doctor, who thinks I'm still behaving erratically. I have no idea what I said to make them believe this, but they sign me off for another three months. Probation clearly believes I'm pulling a fast one and send me to see a psychiatrist in London. They say it's because they care about my wellbeing, but I think it's actually because my union rep has mentioned that I am likely to be entitled to claim for an industrial injury. It's a nice change for the Probation Service to be shitting themselves. I've crashed the car twice in a month, once into a post (I'm sure it had moved) and once into another car in the car park. I'm covered in bruises as I keep falling over.

Having lived in London for years, I'd normally be excited to go and have a look at my old haunts; but right now, feeling agoraphobic, I would rather stay at home. I'm nervous – both about meeting the psychiatrist and about the trip itself. Tom, like the Probation Service, thinks I'm perfectly all right and has been quite oblivious to my new and strange behaviour.

He is just relieved that I have stopped crying and he's enjoying coming home to a clean house and a hot dinner. Beyond this, he feels all is well, apart from our being skint.

Ready for the trip in a smart outfit, I get on my way. Usually, I'm adept at navigating the tube, but on this occasion I'm dithering between the District and Circle Line, unsure which train to get on. I spot what I think is the right train but remain on the platform wondering whether or not to get on. At the last moment I make a jump for it, just as the doors are closing. I have completely mistimed it… You know those moments that are only a few seconds but feel like an eternity? The doors of the tube have closed on my face. My body is still on the platform. I can feel the doors press hard on my cheeks and in the carriage the eyes of the shocked passengers are all on me. A couple of people attempt to prise the doors open. I try to pull my face out, but the doors have closed tighter around my cheeks, and wedged in I can hear the train firing up to move out of the station. Panicking and shouting 'Help!', I make one last effort and yank my face out of the train before it speeds off. Those other passengers on the platform next to me are staring in disbelief and quickly move away from me. My face really hurts. I catch the next train and dash to my appointment.

I'm a bit late now so run straight in. The psychiatrist starts with easy questions like how high my caseload is. He looks surprised when I tell him and asks again to make sure. He continues to look shocked when I tell him the details of the offenders I've been working with, and he gasps when I tell him I haven't had supervision for over a year. I have never had in-depth, clinical supervision in my whole career. Talking to the psychiatrist is the first time I've spoken about the fur-lined van since it happened. I'd forgotten all about it until this point, but his kindly face and probing questions provide a release. I tell him all about Trevor through sobs.

Throughout the interview the psychiatrist looks at me intently, like he's looking deep into my soul. He is quiet throughout, allowing me to speak. I'm thinking, *I know what technique you're using*. Afterwards, I go straight to the loo and look in the mirror. I have a large ring of black oil around my face from the doors of the tube.

The psychiatrist diagnoses me with PTSD and declares I will never be fit to return to probation.

There it is. I feel sick again.

I can't go back. While I had considered leaving before, going potty wasn't part of the plan.

15

What Probation Is Like Now

The work we do with this often-unseen group, those who desperately need to be managed to avoid causing further harm, is our core passion. These people require oversight to spot risks and support to connect them with partner agencies that can prevent further deterioration in their wellbeing and behaviour. Despite the emotional toll of working with individuals in tough circumstances, we remain committed. We face constant challenges: staff shortages, lack of resources, shifting demands, and performance measures that often change with the political winds. But the reason we do this work is simple. We believe in the power of mindset and behaviour change. Every offence has a trigger point, a moment that leads to harmful actions. By helping individuals identify and understand this process, we can redirect their thinking and ultimately reduce the number of future victims. This work is not easy or quick. It takes time and dedication. The results may not be instant, but we see progress. Reducing the risk of harm, even if the offender's behaviour doesn't immediately change, means we're creating a safer community. We can't ignore this group of people; if we don't help them change, we won't ever achieve the society we all want to live in. Our passion for this work remains strong, no matter the obstacles we face.

'Dave', Probation Officer since 1995

***

Sitting on a packed train, the silence is striking. Every passenger is lost in their own world, eyes fixed on glowing screens. I can't eavesdrop on conversations; there are no whispered exchanges between lovers; couples sit mutely beside each other. I lament what I see – we've stopped being curious about those around us, choosing instead to scroll through the lives of those we'll never meet. I give in and join them, glancing at my phone, before turning to the notebook in my lap, filled with notes made from the real conversations I've had over the past week.

It's 2025, ten years since I left probation. I haven't written so intensely since then, when notekeeping was so central to my work. In my darkest hours, trying to make sense of it all, I'd record details from work, conversations and images, before filing them away in the back of my mind once again. The written notes lay idle for years, waiting for me to regain the strength to read them and, indeed, share them here.

This trip up and down the country hasn't been to visit prisoners from my former life but rather to speak with forty-four of the Probation Officers who now supervise them. I've met professionals committed to protecting the public and the rehabilitation of those who have endangered us all. Their

WHAT PROBATION IS LIKE NOW

stories are no less harrowing than the ones shared by the people they work with. They've spoken through tears brought on by stress, described their breakdowns, suicide attempts and the crushing sense of being unsupported and undervalued. Though I'd never met any of them before, it feels like a homecoming. These are my people – their gallows humour, their pathos, and a story involving a man and his 'relationship' with a Golden Retriever. They exude warmth and familiarity, bleak but comforting.

This final chapter is for them, the details all provided by staff I have spoken with and backed up with available research. For everyone who has told me it's a 'shit show', the most common description, this is for you. I hope I can do you the justice you deserve.

***

The Probation Service used to be a quietly competent pillar of the criminal justice system – understated, effective, and internationally respected. As of March 2025, it is responsible for supervising 241,540 offenders, yet, despite its central role within the criminal justice system, it flies under the radar of social consciousness. Attracting little public interest, it is beholden to the whims of the political party of the day and has been subject to regular, sweeping changes. Today, it's limping along, chronically understaffed, hollowed out, and increasingly unsafe. The number of Serious Further Offences committed by individuals under probation supervision has increased by thirty-three per cent in 2023/24 (HM Inspectorate Probation).

For decades, probation policy has been steered by whatever slogan fits the political mood. Tony Blair's 'Tough on Crime' crusade ballooned the prison population by sixty-six per cent between 1995 and 2009. By 2012, the UK had the most privatised prison system in Europe. Each new government seems to follow the same script: make sweeping changes, watch them fall apart, then blame the last lot. But no one before had quite the same fatal impact upon the service as Chris Grayling.

In 2012, Grayling was appointed Justice Secretary and Lord Chancellor, the first non-lawyer to hold the role in over 400 years. He had an agenda that he was determined to pursue at any cost. Despite warnings of its possible disastrous outcomes from experts, unions and even his own department, Grayling pushed through his 'Transforming Rehabilitation' reforms in 2014. Half of the Probation Service was 'adopted' by the Civil Service, who were clearly also reluctant about the union. As the newest member of the family, the Probation Service didn't receive the same benefits or recognition as everyone else and continues to be an afterthought. The other half of the Probation Service was privatised, creating Community Rehabilitation Companies (CRCs), at a cost of £500 million to the public. With no standard practices or proper training, the CRCs handled low- and medium-risk offenders, including, with disastrous consequences, the perpetrators of domestic abuse.

The new CRC contracts were primarily won by multinational service companies (Serco was back again) who saw an opportunity to maximise profits by replacing qualified staff with digital solutions, many of which failed to deliver the intended results. Experienced officers were made redundant, leaving an understaffed, under-skilled workforce. One national inspection found offices operating on only fifty-five per cent of their workforce, yet resources were still wasted with duplicate staff from both teams attending multi-agency meetings. Supervision suffered, paperwork increased, and risk to the public grew.

The consequences have been deadly. According to a report by HM Inspectorate of Probation, in 2019–20, seventy-four individuals under probation supervision were convicted of murder, fifty-four of rape, twenty-five of manslaughter, and eighteen of attempted murder – among other serious offences. These numbers are shocking enough, but behind some of them is a newly qualified, twenty-three-year-old Probation Officer, someone who entered the job wanting to make a positive difference. With no real experience, no support, and no business managing such high-risk cases, they were left to supervise dangerous individuals alone. Now, they must live with the life-changing weight of responsibility for their poor decisions: mistakes made not through negligence, but through political neglect of the probation system.

The high-profile murder of Terri Harris, her two children John and Lacey, and their friend Connie in 2021 by Damien Bendall – who had been released on licence and was being supervised by overworked, inexperienced staff – was a shocking illustration of a system under strain. The case of Zara Aleena in 2022 only deepened that sense of failure. Her killer, Jordan McSweeney, had been released from prison just nine days before he sexually assaulted and murdered her as she walked home from an evening out. A subsequent watchdog report described his case as 'symptomatic of much broader issues', pointing to chronic understaffing, poor communication, and a dangerous lack of oversight.

After six catastrophic years, the Probation Service was quietly re-nationalised in 2021, but not before it had been swallowed up under the banner of HM Prison and Probation Service (HMPPS) in 2017 by Liz Truss, a move more akin to a bad makeover than a reform. The merger blurred boundaries, drained budgets (complete with yet another round of 'DO NOT use the old letterhead'), and left the Probation Service playing second fiddle to its bigger, louder partner, the prison system. Meanwhile, the architect of the mess, Chris Grayling, was made a Lord in 2024. As with other politicians who have made terrible mistakes, he suffered no personal repercussions, leaving devastation in his wake. A once respected and, crucially, well-functioning public body – something that can't be said for many of them at this point – was left in tatters.

'Failing Grayling' became a byword for ministerial incompetence. His most catastrophic probation reforms fell within a range of howlers including awarding a £13.8 million ferry contract to a firm with no ships, banning books being sent to prisoners from friends and family (later ruled unlawful since books are essential to rehabilitation), and presiding over a rail timetable collapse that led to thousands of cancelled trains. His blunders have allegedly cost the taxpayer over £2.75 billion.

To put this into context, in the early 2000s, drug intervention programmes (DIPs) across the country were running at a cost of £150 million per year.* The highly successful interventions included multi-agency liaison between the NHS, the Probation Service, drugs services and the police and, in many areas where it was in operation, acquisitive crime was reduced by forty per cent. Funding was eventually cut altogether and the schemes folded. £2.75 billion would have kept all those policies going for nearly two decades. In some areas, such as London, drugs schemes have never fully recovered and drugs counselling for the most committed users consists of a weekly meeting with a young psychology graduate with lots of enthusiasm but little experience. Most users genuinely want to come off, but they need robust and consistent intervention.

A recruitment drive for new staff soon followed renationalisation. With entry requirements that included a degree from female-dominated subjects such as psychology the Probation Service is now predominantly staffed by young women.† There are reports that in some offices there are no male officers *at all*, offering less diversity of opinion and sensibility, not to mention the ability to safely and appropriately match offenders to officers.

In view of the lack of experienced staff, many young officers have been promoted to management positions without ever having supervised a high-risk offender themselves, creating a 'blind leading the blind' environment. This is in stark

---

* Russell Webster, 'Why the Drugs Intervention Programme is no longer fit for purpose', 23 February 2012: https://www.russellwebster.com/why-the-drugs-intervention-programme-is-no-longer-fit-for-purpose/.

† HMPPS workforce figures for March 2025 showed that 75.6 per cent of probation staff were women.

contrast to how it was before privatisation, when we shadowed experienced officers and weren't allowed to supervise high-risk offenders alone until we'd been qualified for over two years. It was unheard of for officers to be promoted to management positions unless they had been working with offenders for many years. They needed the variety of exposure to know how to respond to crises quickly and competently. I know of offices where teams of twelve are now down to four and where staff with twenty years' experience are being supervised by an ambitious twenty-five-year-old with less than two years, post-qualifying experience.

As I was putting the finishing touches to this book, official documents were leaked showing a 10,000-person shortfall in probation staff, as reported by the BBC. One Probation Officer was quoted as saying: 'It's infuriating when some of us are being told it's our fault we're not doing enough and that we need to up our game, but actually the workload is sky high'. In February 2025, the Ministry of Justice admitted that officers had been 'asked to do too much for too long', leading to 'missed warning signs'.* The situation has been compounded by the early release scheme, where between September 2024 and March 2025 a further 26,456 prisoners have been released, easing the prison population but increasing probation caseloads.

There are similar tales in prisons, again woefully short-staffed. A prison officer friend of mine recently reported that

---

* Sima Kotecha, 'Leaked report shows 10,000 shortfall in probation staff', BBC News, 20 August 2025: https://www.bbc.co.uk/news/articles/cy7yj0gkl3zo

he looks out of his office window at 8 a.m. to see a long line of 4x4s, which resembles the school run, instead of what it is – parents dropping off their eighteen-year-old prison officer children at work. The £30,000 starting salary, requirement of just five GCSEs and flexibility to apply at seventeen and start work on your eighteenth birthday makes it an attractive proposition for young people. Few truly comprehend the dangerous environment into which they are setting foot and staff retention has become a significant issue.

In view of staff shortages and added bureaucracy the focus on genuine rehabilitation has been lost. One-size-fits-all interventions have replaced the personalised, relationship-based supervision that once helped people change. Instead of building trust and tailoring support to individual needs, staff now rely on checklists and generic exercises, tools that are ill-suited to the complexity of human behaviour and the criminal mind. This impersonal approach creates a revolving door of reoffending, where those with the potential to change fall through the cracks. Meaningful rehabilitation and personalised supervision to help effect long-term change have been sacrificed in favour of following rigid scripts from handbooks, box-ticking, copy-and-paste care, and monthly phone calls. An in-person rapport is impracticable in these circumstances, meaning, quite simply, that the compassion that was at the heart of probation is long gone. Many managers report that when inspecting files, the cutting and pasting is so flagrant that there hasn't even been a change of name.

High staff turnover has further eroded the trusting relationships that are built over time and are essential for lasting change, with clients having several Probation Officers over the course of an Order. One person told me she had just finished training the eighteenth new staff member in two years – an exhausting task that takes up much of her time – only for most of them to hastily leave, with staff shortages remaining constant.

In 2023, aware of the lack of diversity of officers and staff shortages, the Probation Employment Pathway (PEP, they love a three-letter acronym) was introduced. Encouragingly, they are including the employment of ex-offenders, who at least have some understanding of the system. They have proven that they have been rehabilitated and want to make a positive contribution. The entry requirements otherwise include five GCSEs and a starting wage of £28,000, about the same as a job at Lidl. If they want to progress to being fully qualified there is online academic training provided in tandem with working on the job, but tutors report that cameras are switched off, children are playing in the background, people are wearing their pyjamas, or the course is being undertaken in the middle of a busy office at work, where only forty per cent of work time is spent. Therefore, further opportunities to learn through observation are considerably curtailed. The training course is tough, and many people drop out. The latest figures indicate that of around 1,500 who started the course, ninety had dropped out within the first three months of training.[*] While this may not seem like much, colleagues have told me anecdotally that dropouts skyrocket after six months; unfortunately, statistics are unavailable for this period. If they do

---

[*] 'Response to Ruth Cadbury MP's question regarding Probation Service resignations to Edward Argar, then Secretary of State for Justice', 22 April 2024: https://questions-statements.parliament.uk/written-questions/detail/2024-04-16/2202.

manage to complete the training, some take advantage of their free degree and move on. (Training is to degree level, but there are no student fees.) As probation is now part of the civil service, they can then sidestep into a job with less responsibility but the same pay.

Even at admin levels, where high levels of responsibility and knowledge of systems are also required, the government was embarrassed to discover that when they raised the minimum wage, probation staff fell well short of it.

Advertisements for new recruits promise plenty of support, but the reality doesn't bear this out. In August 2024, Justice Secretary Shabana Mahmood, who appears to have little understanding of the complexities of working with sex offenders, downgraded rehabilitation for high and very high-risk individuals, by dropping the role from a Band 4 to a Band 3 pay grade.[*] This has resulted in pay cuts of up to £10,000 for those who deliver the Horizon programme. Horizon, a respected sex offender treatment programme, has traditionally been handled by specialist Probation Officers, many with decades of experience. The pay cut has prompted an exodus of experienced staff.

Supervising sex offenders wasn't in the job description for new recruits. When some have refused, due to their own histories of abuse, they have been forced to disclose personal

---

[*] Jessica Bradley, 'Ministry of Justice Downgrading of Sex Offender Rehabilitation Will Have "Catastrophic Effect" on Public Safety, Union Warns', *Byline Times*, 8 July 2024: https://bylinetimes.com/2024/07/08/ministry-of-justice-downgrades-sex-offender-rehabilitation-leaving-will-have-catastrophic-effect-on-public-safety-union-warns/.

trauma at work. One person told me they had never spoken about it before, not even to their own family, but felt pressured to share it in the workplace. They were offered two days of counselling to 'get over it'. They soon left the service.

The probation union Napo has called the move a 'catastrophic' threat to public safety, pointing out that experienced staff are far more likely to spot early signs of risk that could otherwise be missed. While working with sex offenders can be one of the most rewarding and impactful areas within probation, many new recruits feel unprepared and deeply uncomfortable taking on this role without proper support or training.

Recent updates to job descriptions now reflect the reality of the client group new recruits will be expected to work with. The result of this has been telling. In some areas, the latest recruitment drive has resulted in zero applicants. I've been told that in more expensive parts of the country, in particular London and the south, the combination of low pay and high risk simply makes the job unviable. In the north, my friend Dave tells me,

> Our newly recruited POs in training are rushed through rigorous schemes of work from the university course to court placements to 'on the job' training, which basically means they're handed some cases. For our unqualified new recruits, uncertain what they applied for, they hit the ground at speed, immediately working with the full range of offenders in case management, programme delivery or court, despite having no previous experience or training. They come

out exhausted and frazzled… Thankfully though there are signs that, although knackered before they begin, more newly qualified officers are staying in the job!

At the start of this book, I introduced you to the domestic abuser, 'Mr Brown'. A typical (and heavily edited) contact log written by an inexperienced officer might now look something like this:

1 April: Mr Brown tells me that his wife is a 'scheming bitch'. He insists he's done nothing wrong and claims he wouldn't be in this situation if it weren't for her.

25 April: Some seemingly positive news – Mr Brown and his wife are back together. They're taking things slowly and going on dates again.

2 May: Mr Brown reports that Mrs Brown has been 'nagging' him again, but he hasn't reacted. He says he's proud of his progress and that their relationship is growing stronger.

30 May: Mr and Mrs Brown are now fully back together. Mr Brown has moved out of his parents' house and returned home. Everything appears to be going well, and based on this, I reassessed his risk from medium to low. I'm genuinely happy for them both.

In an effort to build a positive working relationship with Mr Brown, the inexperienced Probation Officer has failed to exercise appropriate professional curiosity, taking Mr Brown's version of events at face value.

In reality, it's highly unlikely that within eight weeks Mr Brown has shifted his perspective from seeing Mrs Brown as a 'scheming bitch' to viewing her as an equal partner. The officer should have continued to work with him, addressing concerns about positive relationships. Mrs Brown should have been contacted through victims' support to check whether she is safe and not being coerced. A victim support officer should then have been engaged to ensure she was receiving proper care. It's likely to have taken months of abuse before Mrs Brown felt able to call the police in the first place. Now, she's receiving no support, while Mr Brown rightly believes he can manipulate the system without consequence. Far from reducing his risk, it has actually increased.

Staff shortages are also acutely apparent when it comes to mentoring new recruits. Trainees are given a handbook full of supervision checklists and prescribed exercises to use with clients. In theory, it's meant to guide good practice; in reality, it's often ignored. But even so, there's an unspoken expectation that supervision will follow a one-size-fits-all formula – far removed from the nuanced, person-centred approach that once defined probation work.

This highlights a core tension in modern probation practice: inexperienced officers are often eager to foster positive relationships with those they supervise, yet the system itself is deeply risk averse. Recalls to prison have increased by forty-four per cent, with one in three individuals being returned to custody. If Mr Brown had said, 'I'm thinking of hitting Mrs Brown,' it's likely he would have been recalled immediately. Yet if he says the right things, it's likely he'll get what he wants.

Unlike the courts, probation recalls allow an individual to be sent back to prison without due legal process. There's no hearing or cross-examination to find out the offender's point of view – just a decision made by the officer, who effectively becomes judge and jury. It takes the push of an automated button to have someone recalled, when in the past recall was done rarely and was based upon a difficult and soul-searching decision made after discussion with management. It can now be used easily and is an effective tool to reduce the community caseload. As a result, those familiar with the system learn quickly that honesty carries a high cost. There's no safe space to admit slip-ups with drugs or to discuss dangerous thoughts. Yet failure is a natural part of learning, and without room for honesty, genuine rehabilitation becomes even more elusive.

To save time and reduce court waiting lists, even the bedrock of probation, the Pre-Sentence Report, has been significantly compromised. In 2012–13, 184,000 sentences were imposed with the aid of a PSR as opposed to approximately 99,006 in 2024.* Cases are adjourned for two to three weeks for the preparation of a PSR and the offender interviewed at least once while they are either on bail or on

---

* Stephen Whitehead, 'The changing use of pre-sentence reports', Centre for Justice Innovation, July 2018; *Offender management statistics quarterly: October to December 2024*, HM Prison & Probation Service, 24 April 2025.

remand in custody. Since 2017, most reports have been replaced by Fast Delivery Reports (FDRs) produced the same day, often by unqualified staff, after one brief interview. With no time for background checks, trust-building or verifying information, the quality of these reports has suffered. There is a current trend for an increase in the number of requests for Pre-Sentence Reports again, but nowhere near the quantities of yesteryear.

A rise in custodial sentences as judges lack sufficient information to consider alternatives has ensued. This cost-cutting move has backfired: the prison population is at an all-time high, with £2.5 billion now being spent on new facilities.

In view of the staff crisis, the integrity of community sentencing has also weakened, with sentencers often feeling confused about the range and efficacy of sentences now being offered. The various programmes and rehabilitation activities confuse all within the criminal justice system, the judiciary, probation, advocates, prosecution and the clients themselves. The Ministry of Justice appears committed to producing constant soundbites, name changes and three-letter abbreviations, of which there are now 839 (it was therapeutic to count them), which makes it impossible to keep up with what Probation Officers are talking about much of the time.

Pre-Sentence Reports formed the basis for sentence planning. The requests for reports remains relatively high in some courts, particularly those staffed by experienced officers, and I have heard of examples of an increase in requests for PSRs again since 2023, with a duty to request safeguarding checks from social care. I was pleased to note that some of the traditional practices remain, with barristers continuing to have the 'word of the day', which must be included in every defence case, and Probation Officers still using some of the traditional codes that describe what an offender is *really* like. Including:

> 'He claims' actually means: *This is what he said, but I know he's lying.*
>
> 'He reports' actually means: *This is what he said, and I think he's telling the truth.*
>
> 'He alleges' means: *He's blaming the victim.*
>
> 'He confirms' means: *I know this is true, I confirmed it myself.*
>
> 'I have liaised with several agencies' means: *I tried to phone some people, but nobody answered.*
>
> 'I have liaised with his school, his GP and his social worker' means: *I actually have done this.*
>
> 'This is his first *reported* offence' means: *He hasn't got any previous convictions, but we all know he's been bang at it for years.*
>
> 'He is of previous good character' means: *Bless him, he really hasn't ever done anything before.*

'He lacks the mental capacity' means: *The poor man is really dim.*

'He would find it difficult to engage with a community-based order' means: *Send him down.*

'In my view a robust community order would reduce his risk' means: *I know he's been really naughty, but please oh please don't send him to prison.*

These accepted nuances and 'codes' still make those who practise them smile, but more importantly the hidden meanings in these reports are helpful to sentencers, who ultimately decide the fate of the defendant.

During the most recent national inspection, every area in the country – except South Tyneside and Gateshead – was rated as 'inadequate' or 'requires improvement', particularly when it comes to assessing risk of harm and keeping people safe. Other areas are now turning to South Tyneside and Gateshead to understand the secret of their success. The irony of it is that even they don't seem entirely sure how they achieved it.

In October 2023, facing severe prison overcrowding, Alex Chalk introduced the End of Custody Supervised Licence scheme. Initially, prisoners were to be released eighteen days early – but this was quickly extended to sixty days, without any clear forward planning. By January 2024, thirty per cent of released prisoners were homeless. With only an £89.52 discharge grant and, in some cases, a tent provided by the prison, these individuals were left with no housing, no job prospects and no real hope. Unsurprisingly, reoffending rates soared. Some prisons reported receiving an average of 700 recalled offenders per year* – people who had either breached their licence conditions or committed new crimes.

Remember Andrew, the burglar? When he was released, we were ready for him. He had accommodation lined up, a job waiting and regular support from a drug worker. He had a real shot at turning his life around. When he admitted to trying heroin, I didn't recall him to prison, I allowed him the opportunity to be really pissed off and angry with himself. We increased his level of appointments with a drug worker and, with his permission, drug tested him more regularly. He made the decision not to do it again. Our cheap but effective intervention saved the taxpayer over £50,000 in prison costs in one year.

Soon after taking office, Keir Starmer announced plans to tackle the prison overcrowding crisis by releasing more prisoners early. These surprise changes came with almost no extra support for probation, who overnight had an influx of new clients, and middle managers were expected to cope with the changes that were sprung on them, apparently from nowhere. It has only added to the pressure on a service already stretched to its limits. While efforts have been made towards imposing shorter community sentences, and only supervising the high-risk cases, the real issues haven't gone away. Probation Officers have deep concerns that short community sentences for those deemed as 'medium' risk pose real dangers, particularly for

---

* See 'HMP Peterborough (Men)', HM Inspectorate of Prisons, 9 April 2024: https://hmiprisons.justiceinspectorates.gov.uk/hmipris_reports/hmp-peterborough-men/.

those convicted of domestic abuse offences, as left without robust intervention, their risk of committing serious harm can be increased rather than addressed.

What we need is a complete overhaul of the justice system. I realise this sounds daunting. But long-term thinking, proper investment and a real focus on reducing reoffending might one day make for fewer criminals and a safer public. Building more prisons isn't the solution. Prison doesn't stop crime. It's just a sticking plaster. As a society, we need to take a hard look at our attitudes to incarceration.

Britain's high prison population can be attributed to punitive public attitudes, often rooted in ignorance about their cost and ineffectiveness or the benefits and relative cheapness of alternatives, opportunistic politicians who exploit these sentiments for electoral gain, sensationalist media that inflame public opinion and pressure politicians to act punitively, all enforced by a judiciary that lacks confidence in non-custodial options.

The Probation Service, a once proud profession, has been reduced to spreadsheets and panic; a workforce too new to know what good supervision even looks like; and a revolving door of reoffending that keeps on turning.

Probation doesn't have to fail, but it has been failed, from the top down.

***

This chapter has been the hardest to write. The despair and frustration felt by the staff I've spoken to is unambiguous. It is at the core of every conversation.

Desperate to end on a positive note, I asked everyone I spoke to if there was *anything* good about probation these days. Most responded with a heartfelt *no*, struggling to find even a flicker of light. But there were a few sparks: new officers, inexperienced, yes, but with a natural feel for the job, who can assess risk and respond with quiet, competent care. In some areas, 'levelling-up' funds are being spent on housing for people coming out of prison and some probation areas have begun to employ accommodation officers again to facilitate this.

There's also a far better understanding of mental health now than there was in my day. There is growing awareness of things like acquired brain injury, which can affect cognitive ability and behaviour long after the original trauma. In 2018, research by 'Brainkind', formerly the Disabilities Trust, indicated that up to sixty per cent of serving prisoners could have an acquired brain injury caused by violence perpetrated against them as children and sixty-four per cent of female prisoners, who have also been victims of domestic violence. Some areas are working in partnership with Public Health England, who are offering sessions to explore the effects of abuse, bereavement and PTSD.

But really, it was my two friends, Katie and Dave, working in different parts of the country, who brought proper optimism.

Dave is still fully committed. 'It's got to work,' he tells me. 'We're the only people who can do this.'

And though Katie hasn't worked directly with offenders for many years, she is still employed by the service working in policy and said simply, 'I love probation.' Despite the stress, the terrible management and the massive caseload that nearly broke me, I agree. Others have said the same, or its more wistful cousin: 'I *used* to love probation.'

Katie, though, is *still* in love with it. She's been in the service since the nineties and has weathered every storm. She believes the tide might finally be turning, that somewhere in government, people are starting to see the value of probation and its person-centred approach. The power of listening, building trust, treating people with dignity and recognising that it serves a purpose.

She and Dave both see hints of progress: pilot schemes supporting middle managers (long overdue), multi-agency hubs with mental health teams and police working side by side, and even former clients returning – not for supervision this time, but as colleagues. Dave describes that after an utterly demoralising few years, upper management are using constructive terms and phrases to describe their plans for probation, and he is finally allowing himself to believe them and feel optimistic too.

I've spent the past month speaking to probation staff at all levels and found inspiring people everywhere I went. They all want the same thing: to be cared for and treated with respect by their employer, and to have the time to share that same ethos with their clients. Crucially, they expect at least to be consulted before change is hurled at them, and to be involved in that change. They are the experts. Ministers, you need to stop going over their heads and talk to them: to the staff, not just the managers. Stop sending out staff survey forms, get off your laptop and go and see them personally. Learn about how to communicate from a Probation Officer. Probation is one of the most important public sector organisations in the country. When it's run well, it reduces crime, helps victims and it's cheap. It has the power to change lives, not just for individuals but for entire communities. Amid the despair and cynicism, I choose to treasure Dave and Katie's hopes. And wouldn't it be lovely if they turned out to be right?

As for me, accepting that returning to life as a Probation Officer would probably finish me off, I now massage people for a living. Most of the time they're half-asleep, which suits me fine. I wanted to work with people, but I didn't want to listen to them talk anymore, so I just drift off into my own little world, reminiscing and concocting recipes in my mind. It's just so Zen.

There's a chance I've massaged you. I travel all over the place, into lovely offices where the employers care about their staff and invest in their wellbeing (clearly none of them are in the public sector) or to muddy fields at festivals, massaging cheerful, slightly wobbly people who've had too many ciders and think I'm some kind of wizard.

I still listen to people's problems, but they are of a different order of magnitude. Like the woman who couldn't get out of her husband's Lamborghini because, in her words, 'My bum's too big and the door's too small.'

Or someone else confiding: 'I think my dog is psychic.'

I miss my old probation clients, the chaos, the emergencies, seeing them adapt and commit to change. Even the murderers and the rapists – to acknowledge their risks and to protect the public, but also to see the humanity in them. They are not one-dimensional baddies. Some have done terrible things, things that are unforgiveable, but even those who have committed the most heinous of crimes have another side. A side that is likeable and kind, that is redeemable, a side that needs to be encouraged, bought to the forefront, a side that can eventually take over and suppress the part of them that wants to cause harm. Consider the story of Steve Gallant, who was convicted of the brutal murder of Barrie Jackson in 2005. Nothing can ever bring Barrie back or erase the pain his family has endured. His loss is permanent, and the grief immeasurable.

And yet, years later, on his very first day out on release after serving a seventeen-year sentence, Gallant did something no one could have expected. During the 2019 London Bridge attack, he confronted the terrorist Usman Khan, who was armed with two knives and wearing a fake suicide vest. Gallant's actions that day were nothing short of heroic. He very likely saved the lives of many innocent people, risking his own in the process.

Today, he works to help others find a path forward. He not only fundraises for the Howard League, but also runs a housing scheme for ex-offenders in Northampton, supporting their rehabilitation and giving them a second chance: something he has fought hard to earn himself.

His story is a powerful reminder that even those who have caused great harm are capable of remorse, courage and compassion.

There are many other examples of ex-offenders who now work tirelessly to improve the lives of others.

Less dramatic but worth a mention is Steve, the murderer. He's a kind and considerate neighbour. Everyone in his block of flats has got clean dustbins and their communal garden is something to behold! Ben the rapist (last time I call him that, I promise) works and is still married to a very happy Stella.

People can change.

Like lots of ex-probation staff I've spoken to, I'll always be one at heart. It becomes part of you. All the people I met, the stories I heard, the brave and resilient people who have completely turned their lives around. Those like Stella, who have careers of their own helping others with her unique insight into how they feel. My lovely former colleagues, who still invite me to the Christmas do and are now sick of me asking them questions for this book! But now? My only 'client' is Tom. I didn't want to lose my skills, and I've got the time to devote and concentrate on him. I've used every trick in the probation book, from pro-social modelling, motivational interviewing and positive reinforcement. And it's paid off. He makes the bed, doesn't leave skidders and washes up after us both. I never did shout as that approach tends not to pay off, so he might never have known the extent of my despair, but he has, in fact, changed. He is living proof that, with a low caseload, a steady supply of love and a bit of time, probation works.

Acknowledgements

I'd like to thank my family, in particular Kim and Lottie, who put up with me when I was a stressed-out Probation Officer and subsequently, when I was going on and on about this book for at least three years. My parents, for making me speak properly and taking me to lots of National Trust houses, and of course, for just being glorious!

I'd like to thank my probation friends from around the country who have let me pester them with questions while doing research and plunder some of their stories. Especially Dave H – you are a legend. Dave, Jo C and Anita for your help and Mark S, for inviting me to the Probation Service Christmas do every year still. Katie R and Nick S for your read-throughs and information about probation now. To Marshy for your anecdotes and support. To Pauline M, for your anecdotes about the power of education and employment. To Steve and Sarah for being great neighbours.

Cheryl M and Rebecca C for the confidence, reading and rereading at the beginning of this journey. To Pam L for the huge number of read-throughs and corrections more recently.

To Jo A, who is convinced that I'm going to be famous. Thank you for your faith. If I get invited to anything interesting or a free dinner, I'll take you.

To my lovely agent Daisy Parente who took a punt on me even though I'd never written anything before. And to my editor Cecilia Stein and her assistant Hannah Haseloff for their guidance and reining in of my knob jokes.

To Julie, thank you for lending me your dad, Ray Bellamy, when he was alive. He was the best mentor and taught me that anything is possible. Without him I'd never have been a Probation Officer, gone to university twice or indeed written this book.